THE TRIED & TRUE COOKBOOK

THE
TRIED & TRUE
COOKBOOK

150 QUICK AND EASY RECIPES FOR BUSY FAMILIES

ALYSSA RIVERS

Publisher Mike Sanders
Art & Design Director William Thomas
Editorial Director Ann Barton
Senior Editor Brook Farling
Development Editor Christy Wagner
Senior Designer Jessica Lee
Food Photographer Alyssa Rivers
Lifestyle Photographers Erin Thunell,
Angie Monson, and Alexia Privitera
Proofreaders Lisa Starnes, Monica Stone
Indexer Beverlee Day

First American Edition, 2024
Published in the United States by DK Publishing
1745 Broadway, 20th Floor, New York, NY 10019

The authorized representative in the EEA is Dorling
Kindersley Verlag GmbH. Arnulfstr. 124, 80636 Munich,
Germany

Library of Congress number: 2023941694
ISBN: 978-0-7440-9093-2

DK books are available at special discounts when
purchased in bulk for sales promotions, premiums, fund-
raising, or educational use. For details, contact
SpecialSales@dk.com

Printed and bound in China

www.dk.com

CONTENTS

SIDE DISHES

DINNER

DESSERTS

CELEBRATIONS

SEASONINGS AND SAUCES

ACKNOWLEDGMENTS

Wow! What a ride this has been. I could not have done it without my people.

First to my husband and kiddos: To my husband, you believed in me when I had the crazy idea to start my blog. To my children, you are the reason why I work so hard and keep going every single day. You give me such strength, and I am so proud of you and how you have turned out despite the challenges we have faced. I love each of you so much, and I love the adventures we go on and the memories we make.

To my amazing team: This cookbook wouldn't be possible without you. Jenny, you were seriously the backbone of this cookbook. You worked so hard behind the scenes, organized everything so it went smoothly, and made this entire cookbook possible. April, "Apes," you were by my side during every photoshoot, helping me style the food perfectly, adding the "sprinks," and making each recipe beautiful. I couldn't have done it without you. You kept us laughing and having fun while photographing every single recipe. Amanda and Devyn, my studio team, you are incredible. Thank you for keeping the studio going with your amazing recipe development. You make working in the studio so much fun, and we couldn't have done the photos without your help. To my sisters, Kelsey and Laura. Kelsey, your graphic skills are unmatched. You did such a beautiful job creating the cover for the cookbook. You go above and beyond, and it has been amazing to see your talent shine. Laura, you are our social media mastermind. Your love and commitment to me and our followers means more than you will ever know. Thank you to my team for caring about my blog just as much as I do.

To my team at DK: Thank you to Brook Farling and Christy Wagner for holding my hand through the editing process and to Jessica Lee for making the design look amazing. And I'll be forever in debt to the team at DK

marketing and publicity for making this book shine and getting it into people's hands and making sure it has a place on the shelves.

To my wonderful parents: I have learned to appreciate you even more as I have become a mother myself. We have learned and grown a lot through the challenges during the years. Thank you for always showing up for me when I need you. I can't imagine having to go through some of the things you did with me, but you did, and we made it through, and I am so thankful for that. You have been the best "papa and nans" to my children, and we love you so much!

And of course, to my siblings, Christopher, Laura, and Kelsey: Thank you for being the best Thanksgiving–side dish taste-testers and for so many laughs around the dinner table. I love you all!

To the lifestyle photographers, Angie, Erin, and Alexia: Thanks for helping me capture these pieces of my life for the book. It was fun trekking up to the cabin in the snow, taking pictures in Paris, and having you in my home with me. You were awesome and made my vision come to life.

To my gym family: Thank you for being my escape. We work out to eat and have so much fun together doing it. Thank you for being more than just a gym to go to and for supporting me throughout this journey. I will never forget our cabin "night rides" and all the amazing things we have done together.

To my closest blogging friends: Thank you for being the people who get this crazy blogging world we are part of. Some of my closest friendships are with all of you, and I smile as I think about how we have grown together throughout the years.

To my people: You know who you are. It has taken all of you to get me to this point. There were times in my life I wasn't sure how to move forward. It has been your strength and support that helped me get here. I couldn't do life without you.

And finally, to all my followers and fans: I love you. I have tears in my eyes thinking about how none of this would be possible without you making my recipes and supporting me throughout the years.

HOW TO USE THIS BOOK

Included in this book are 25 new recipes that are exclusive to the book, which means you won't find them anywhere else. All other recipes in the book appear on the Recipe Critic website, and each includes a scannable QR code that links to the recipe on the website. To access the QR code feature, simply open the camera application on your internet-connected device. When you scan the code, a notification will appear that includes a link. Select the link and you will be taken directly to the recipe on the Recipe Critic website, where you'll find the full recipe along with additional preparation tips, recipe reviews, serving suggestions, and other helpful information.

GETTING STARTED

Welcome to *The Tried & True Cookbook*! This cookbook was written with busy families in mind and is perfect for beginners and experienced home cooks alike. In this first section, I begin by sharing a bit about me, my background, and how I came to love cooking and creating delicious, approachable recipes like the ones in this book. Then I give you lots of great information that's helped me as I began cooking, including recommended kitchen equipment, essential ingredients to keep in stock, ingredient substitutions, and helpful cooking tips. By understanding the basic techniques and measurements cooking requires, you'll gain the confidence to tackle any recipe and soon will be impressing your friends and family with the delicious dishes you serve them!

◄ *Food is my love language! Thank you for letting me share it with you! Let's eat!*

INTRODUCTION

Hello there! I'm Alyssa, founder and CEO of The Recipe Critic (therecipecritic.com).

I discovered my love of cooking when I got married in 2003 and had to learn to feed my family. At first, I didn't know where to begin, but my mother-in-law taught me everything she knew about cooking—my husband was used to her delicious home-cooked meals, so I was happy to learn her ways—and she inspired me to create my own dishes. Some of my favorite recipes in this book are from her, and I'm grateful to have learned and developed my passion for cooking from her.

My grandma also was a huge influence on my love of cooking and baking. She cooked from scratch for a big family of eight kids every day. One of my favorite childhood memories is going to her house and smelling her freshly baked bread, and we always looked forward to her mouthwatering meals and warm-from-the-oven cookies. I've included her pancake (**Grandma's Homemade Pancakes,** page 28) and bread (**Grandma's Homemade Bread,** page 54) recipes in this book because I haven't found anything better. She was an amazing cook.

I love connecting with people through my personal experiences, and I'm always willing to share my story because life can be tough and we need each other. It feels good to be genuine instead of presenting a picture-perfect life for social media, and I knew that if I were to publish a cookbook, I wanted it to reflect my real life—authentic, unfiltered, and with its share of challenges. I wouldn't trade my life experiences, difficult or not, for anything.

I grew up in a family of six, with amazing parents whom I appreciate even more now that I have teenagers of my own. My parents always have been supportive, even during tough times, like when I became a young mom at 18 and my first marriage lasted just seven years.

I learned to navigate as a single parent, relying heavily on food stamps and the support of others, which gave me a greater appreciation for those who have to do it all alone. After a few years, I got remarried to my current husband.

During the first summer of my second marriage, we moved from Utah to North Carolina. People back home kept asking me for recipes, so I decided to share them on a blog with some simple photos I took with my phone. I named my site "The Recipe Critic" because the recipes I shared were family-tested and family-approved dishes, with my husband and my kids as my biggest critics. A few months later, one of my Pinterest pins went viral, and I realized that more than just my mom and a few friends were visiting my site. From that point on, I worked tirelessly to build something amazing, from a busy mom's perspective, and that others could relate to, with straightforward, relatable recipes. I started taking my own photos and soon mastered the art of food photography to show home cooks the kinds of dishes they can make in their own kitchens.

I never could have imagined that my blog would become my full-time career, yet it has, with the help of an amazing team of women who have helped grow it from a passion and hobby into a mini culinary empire that is one of the largest food blogs in the country. The Recipe Critic is a trusted resource for more than 10 million home cooks nationwide each month, with quick, affordable, approachable recipes for everyday life. They're the recipes I prepare for my own family, and the dishes have resonated with others.

After all, who has time to cook complicated meals with long lists of complicated ingredients when there's dance practice at 6 p.m. or soccer until 7:30 p.m.? My life is incredibly busy as a mom of four and a business owner, so the recipes I share need to be quick and call for easy-to-find ingredients.

The Tried & True Cookbook features some of my most popular tried and true recipes along with many brand-new recipes that will make it your go-to cookbook for breads, breakfasts, soups and salads, sandwiches, dinners, appetizers, desserts, and more. The nearly 160 restaurant-quality recipes in *The Tried & True Cookbook* will make you confident in your own kitchen, whether you're a beginner cook or more experienced. You can make these recipes with minimal ingredients and often not a lot of time—perfect for hectic weekday meals and celebrations alike.

Turn the page, and you will quickly discover why millions of people return to The Recipe Critic's table—tried and true, and picky-eater approved.

ESSENTIAL KITCHEN TOOLS

Having a well-equipped kitchen makes you a more prepared—and more confident—cook. These simple tools cover a wide range of cooking and baking tasks and will level up your cooking game.

Baking sheet: Essential for baking cookies and dessert bars, a baking sheet is also the go-to pan for roasting savory meats and veggies in the oven.

Blender: A blender effortlessly transforms ingredients into creamy smoothies, sauces, zesty salsas, and even delicate crepe batters.

Cast-iron pan: A must-have in any kitchen, a cast-iron pan seamlessly transitions from the stove top to the oven.

Colander: A reliable colander (also called a *strainer*) effortlessly drains cooked pasta and other ingredients.

Grater: A grater enables you to cook with freshly grated cheese instead of preshredded cheese, which not only has a superior taste but also blends and melts much better.

Knife: A sharp knife is a must in any kitchen. Choose a durable, top-quality knife that will stand the test of time and keep its edge for precise and efficient cooking.

Kitchen shears: This tool is an absolute must. Kitchen shears trim fat from meat, open packages, snip fresh herbs, and cut up food so quickly. Opt for dishwasher-safe shears to make your life so much easier.

Mandoline: Cut down on prep time with a multitasking mandoline that will chop, shred, and slice just about anything. This time-saving tool is a game changer.

Measuring cups: Essential for cooking and baking, measuring cups accurately portion out dry and liquid ingredients. A well-rounded set has 1-cup, ¾-cup, ½-cup, and ¼-cup sizes. For liquids, 1-cup and 4-cup measuring cups are handy.

Measuring spoons: These are necessary for any recipe and enable you to precisely measure ingredients.

Meat thermometer: Say goodbye to undercooked or overcooked meat with the help of a reliable meat thermometer. This tool allows you to check the internal temperature of cooked meat to be sure it's safe to eat.

Mixer: A stand or handheld electric mixer simplifies your baking and cooking in so many ways. A stand mixer is a time-saving tool for hands-free mixing and for recipes that require extended mixing times, such as whipped cream and meringue. It can even shred cooked chicken breasts! A hand mixer is a more compact alternative to a stand mixer that's easy to clean and store.

Mixing bowls: From whisking batters to holding chopped vegetables, mixing bowls are a must in the kitchen. Use large bowls for combining ingredients, medium bowls for veggie prep, and small bowls for whisking sauces and beating eggs.

Muffin pans: These aren't just for baking muffins. They're also perfect for creating individual portions of recipes.

Nonstick pots and pans: A variety of sizes of pots and pans make cooking and cleanup a breeze, with their effortless food release, reduced need for oil or fat, and quick cleaning.

Spatulas: Used for cooking and scraping, rubber or silicone spatulas are the best for mixing ingredients in bowls or pots and pans. Their flexible nature allows them to perfectly bend and scrape every last bit from the bowl.

Salt and pepper grinders: Freshly ground spices seem to deliver more flavor, and high-quality salt and pepper grinders make that happen. Take the effort out of grinding your own spices and consider the convenience of an electric grinder. Trust me, it's worth it!

Tongs: Tongs can be used to flip meat on the grill, assist in frying foods, and serve salads easily. With various sizes available, tongs come to the rescue in countless tasks.

Whisks: Whisks are the quick and easy go-to tool for beating eggs, creating smooth sauces, whisking dressings and gravies, and combining batters.

Wooden spoons: Great for everyday cooking, wooden spoons ensure that your cookware won't get scratched by metal equipment.

PANTRY STAPLES

A well-stocked pantry and spice rack will save you meal-prep time and prevent last-minute grocery store runs. This list of ingredients to keep on hand will ensure you're always prepared to create delicious meals.

All-purpose flour: Essential for baking, all-purpose flour is used in a wide range of recipes, from cakes to breads and beyond.

Baking powder: This leavening agent contains both an acid and a base, ensuring baked goods rise and become light and fluffy.

Baking soda: Another leavening agent, this helps dough rise by releasing carbon dioxide when combined with acidic ingredients.

Beans: I like to have canned cannellini, navy, black, and pinto beans on hand because they are nutritious protein sources that add flavor and texture to soups, salads, and side dishes.

Breadcrumbs: I keep different varieties of breadcrumbs on hand, like Italian, panko, and plain, for breading, coating, and adding a delightful crunch to various dishes.

Brown sugar: Brown sugar adds rich flavor and moisture to baked goods, enhancing both their taste and texture.

Canned tomatoes: I like having cans of diced, stewed, and crushed tomatoes on hand because they are used in many recipes.

Chicken broth: This versatile base for soups, stews, and sauces provides depth and savory goodness to your recipes.

Cocoa powder, unsweetened: Cocoa powder brings a rich, chocolate flavor to baked goods, desserts, and beverages.

Confectioners' sugar: Commonly used for making frostings and glazes and for dusting desserts, confectioners' sugar adds a touch of sweetness and a beautiful finishing touch.

Evaporated milk: This creamy ingredient lends its smoothness to desserts, sauces, and beverages, making them more flavorful and indulgent.

Honey: A natural sweetener that's also a versatile ingredient in baking and cooking, honey adds a distinct sweetness to a wide variety of dishes.

Maple syrup: Another natural sweetener, sweet and rich maple syrup is perfect for drizzling over pancakes, waffles, and desserts.

Olive oil: I like to have regular olive oil on hand for cooking as well as extra-virgin olive oil for uncooked dishes. Olive oil adds a distinct flavor to salads, marinades, and sautés, and provides a touch of Mediterranean charm.

Pasta: Whether it's bowtie, penne, rigatoni, angel hair, or fettuccine, I always like to have some sort of dry pasta noodles on hand.

Rice: White rice complements many dishes. I use long-grain rice in most recipes. Brown rice, a nutritious alternative to white rice, boasts a nutty flavor and works as a base for stir-fries, pilafs, and other side dishes.

Semisweet chocolate chips: Chocolate chips are perfect for adding rich, chocolatey goodness to cookies, cakes, and desserts.

Soy sauce: Originally from China, this savory sauce adds saltiness and umami to Asian dishes and marinades.

Spices and seasonings: Spices to have on hand include ground cinnamon, whole and ground cloves, ground ginger, ground cumin, ground turmeric, garlic powder, onion powder, sweet paprika, crushed red pepper flakes, chili powder, taco seasoning, Italian seasoning, bay leaves, dried basil, dried thyme, dried oregano, dried rosemary, dried dill, lemongrass, salt, and black pepper. Try my **Easy Italian Seasoning** (page 263) and **The Best Homemade Taco Seasoning** (page 265)!

Sugar: A common sweetener used in baking and cooking, granulated sugar provides a touch of sweetness to various recipes and enhances their taste.

Tomato paste: Concentrated tomato paste adds flavor, depth, and richness to sauces, soups, and stews.

Vanilla extract: Vanilla extract enhances the flavor of baked goods and desserts. Opt for pure vanilla extract if you can find it.

Vegetable oil: In addition to olive oil, I like using vegetable oil because it is ideal for frying, sautéing, and baking.

Vinegar: Vinegar is used for dressings, marinades, and sauces. White vinegar, rice vinegar, red wine vinegar, and apple cider vinegar all add acidity and brightness to a variety of dishes.

Worcestershire sauce: This condiment enhances the taste of meats, marinades, and sauces, providing a unique tanginess and depth of flavor to recipes.

Yeast: An essential ingredient for making bread and pizza dough, yeast plays a crucial role in the rising process, resulting in light and fluffy baked goods. Try to keep instant and active dry yeast for different recipe needs.

FOR THE REFRIGERATOR

Butter: I like to have both salted and unsalted butter on hand. They are essential in the kitchen and are used in many recipes.

Buttermilk: Buttermilk adds a subtle tanginess and moisture to baked goods like pancakes, waffles, and biscuits, and contributes to their light and tender texture.

Condiments: Ketchup, mustard, mayonnaise, BBQ sauce; everyday condiments are great to have on hand and use in recipes.

Cream cheese: This creamy and tangy ingredient is perfect for both sweet and savory recipes, adding a velvety texture to cheesecakes, frostings, and more.

Eggs: Versatile eggs add richness, structure, and moisture to various recipes, making them a kitchen staple for baking, cooking, and breakfast dishes.

Frozen vegetables/fruit: It's always a good idea to have frozen vegetables and fruit on hand when they aren't in season. Frozen veggies are great for soups and casseroles. Frozen fruit is perfect in smoothies and pies.

Half-and-half: A blend of milk and cream, half-and-half adds richness and creaminess to drinks, soups, and creamy sauces.

Heavy whipping cream: Heavy whipping cream adds richness and a smooth texture to desserts, sauces, and whipped toppings.

Milk: I use 1% or 2% milk in all my recipes. Because it adds creaminess and moisture, it's a must to always have some in the refrigerator.

Sour cream: Sour cream is used often in dips, dressings, baked goods, and casseroles, making it a must-stock in my fridge.

PRODUCE

Bananas: Bananas are a delicious and healthy fruit I often use in recipes like smoothies and baked goods.

Garlic: I like to have fresh garlic cloves or jarred minced garlic on hand for sauces, marinades, and roasted dishes.

Herbs: Fresh herbs can elevate the flavor and scent of your dishes. My favorites are basil, cilantro, parsley, thyme, rosemary, mint, dill, chives, sage, oregano, lemongrass, and tarragon.

Lemons and limes: These citrus fruits add a tangy and refreshing flavor to drinks and marinades and are often used as a garnish for enhancing the flavor of dishes.

Onions: Onions are used in many recipes. I like white onions for their mild and slightly sweet flavor that's perfect for soups, stir-fries, and sauces. Yellow, red, or green onions are other options.

Spinach: This nutritious leafy green can be added to salads and cooked dishes or blended into smoothies for added vitamins and minerals.

Tomatoes: Tomatoes are used in many recipes. The most common ones I use are Roma and cherry tomatoes.

COOKING SUBSTITUTIONS

You're halfway through fixing dinner and realize you're missing an ingredient. Or you're cooking for friends and need to account for their egg- or sugar-free dietary restrictions. These simple swaps for common ingredients will help keep you on track in the kitchen.

Baking powder: Create your own baking powder to help baked goods rise and become fluffy during baking by combining ½ teaspoon cream of tartar and ¼ teaspoon baking soda for ¾ teaspoon baking powder.

Bread flour: 1 cup all-purpose flour plus 1 teaspoon wheat gluten.

Brown sugar: If you're out of brown sugar, whisk together 1 cup granulated sugar and 1 tablespoon molasses to make 1 cup brown sugar.

Buttermilk: If you don't have buttermilk, you can make 1 cup of a substitute by adding 1 tablespoon white vinegar or lemon juice to a measuring cup and then filling it with enough milk to measure 1 cup. Stir and allow it to sit for a few minutes to curdle slightly before using.

Cake flour: If you're out of cake flour, you can make your own by mixing ¾ cup plus 2 tablespoons all-purpose flour with 2 tablespoons cornstarch for 1 cup cake flour.

Confectioners' sugar: If you're out of confectioners' sugar, blend granulated sugar in a blender or food processor until a powder forms.

Eggs: Several egg substitutions are available for those with food allergies or dietary restrictions. The following are each a substitute for 1 egg:

- 1 tablespoon flaxseed meal mixed with 2 or 3 tablespoons water
- 1 tablespoon chia seeds mixed with 2 or 3 tablespoons water
- ¼ cup mashed banana
- ¼ cup applesauce
- ¼ cup blended silken tofu
- 3 tablespoons aquafaba (the liquid from canned chickpeas [garbanzo beans])

Garlic cloves: 1 clove of garlic = ⅛ teaspoon garlic powder.

Graham cracker crust: If you don't have graham crackers to crush and make into a piecrust, you can use vanilla wafers, shortbread cookies, or vanilla sandwich cookies. Even Teddy Grahams work!

Heavy cream: If you don't have heavy cream, you can use half-and-half as a 1:1 substitute.

Herbs (fresh versus dried): When a recipe calls for 1 tablespoon of a fresh herb, you can substitute 1 teaspoon of the dried herb.

Honey: Agave or pure maple syrup can be used as a substitute for honey in equal amounts.

Lemon juice: If you're out of lemon juice, you can use an equal amount of orange or lime juice because they contribute similar sweet and acidic flavors. This substitution works well in marinades and dressings.

Oil: When baking, you can substitute applesauce, mashed banana, or pumpkin purée for the oil in equal amounts. Melted coconut oil can be used as a substitute for vegetable or canola oil in a 1:1 ratio.

Red wine: If you don't have red wine, you can substitute an equal amount of cranberry juice, grape juice, broth, or water.

Ricotta cheese: Strained cottage cheese can be used as a 1:1 substitute for ricotta cheese.

Sour cream: Greek yogurt or plain yogurt can be used as substitutes for sour cream in a 1:1 ratio.

Sugar: Monkfruit sweetener is a zero-calorie substitute for granulated sugar. You can replace sugar with monkfruit sweetener in a 1:1 ratio in any recipe.

Sweetened condensed milk: Cream of coconut is a dairy-free option to replace sweetened condensed milk in a 1:1 ratio. Another option is heavy cream. Mix 1 cup heavy cream with ¼ cup sugar to achieve a great 1:1 ratio alternative.

White wine: If a recipe calls for white wine, you can use an equal amount of white grape juice, apple juice, broth, or water instead.

HELPFUL TIPS

I'm always jotting down tips that make my life easier in the kitchen, and I want to share some with you! These tips can help all cooks enhance their skills, troubleshoot issues, and explore new flavors and methods.

Practice mise en place: *Mise en place*, a French phrase meaning "everything in its place," is the process of chopping, measuring, and preparing all the ingredients for a recipe in one location, so that when you begin assembly, everything is within reach.

Read the entire recipe before starting: Read through the recipe from start to finish before you begin. This ensures that you are aware of any unexpected resting times or any ingredients or equipment you might be missing.

Measure flour properly: To accurately measure flour, avoid dipping the measuring cup into the container. Instead, use a spoon to scoop the flour into the measuring cup, slightly overfilling it. Then use a flat edge, such as the back of a knife, to level off the flour.

Prevent cutting-board slippage: To prevent your cutting board from slipping while you cut ingredients on it, place a folded, damp paper towel or kitchen towel underneath it. This provides stability and keeps the cutting board securely in place.

Preheat the pan when searing: To achieve a perfect sear on meat, the pan must be hot, so it's important to preheat the pan. To gauge when the pan is hot enough, perform a water test: flick some water into the pan. If the water splits into a few sizzling beads that dance across the surface, it's at the right temperature to add oil. If the water forms a single puddle and sizzles and steams, the pan isn't hot enough yet. If the water splits into numerous small beads that rapidly scatter, it's too hot.

Leave the oven closed: When using the oven for cooking, especially baking, it's crucial to avoid unnecessarily opening the oven door. Even a quick peek can cause a significant drop in oven temperature—up to 100°F (38°C)! This sudden temperature change can make cakes sink and slow the roasting process.

Create a proofing oven: If you're in a hurry for bread dough to rise, you can create a proofing oven. Preheat your oven to the "warm" setting or the lowest possible temperature. Place the bowl with your dough inside the preheated oven. To create steam, use a clean squirt bottle filled with water (avoid using bottles that previously contained cleaning solutions) to spray the bottom and the sides of the oven and then quickly close the door to trap the steam inside. Check the dough after 10 to 20 minutes because this method accelerates the proofing process.

Test cakes for doneness: Testing a cake for doneness by inserting a toothpick in the center is a common method, but you also can press lightly on the center. A properly baked cake should feel spongy, spring back immediately when gently pressed, and leave no lingering indentations from your fingers.

Allow proteins to reach room temperature: Unless otherwise specified in the recipe, let proteins sit at room temperature for about 30 minutes before using in a recipe. This promotes more even cooking, preventing the outer portions from overcooking while waiting for the colder interior parts to reach the desired temperature.

Use a thermometer: When cooking meats, particularly poultry, it is crucial to use a thermometer to check the internal temperature of the thickest part. This ensures that the meat is fully cooked, eliminating the risk of serving undercooked meat that could potentially make someone ill.

Prevent cross-contamination: It's vital to prevent cross-contamination. If your hands, knife, cutting board, or any other utensil come into contact with raw meat or fish, thoroughly wash them before touching anything else. Also wipe down the counter and sink after working with raw meat.

Beware of the temperature danger zone: Bacteria grows rapidly under specific conditions. The "danger zone," or the range between 40°F and 140°F (4.5°C–60°C), where bacterial growth is quickest, must be treated with caution. Leave perishable food at room temperature only for a *maximum of 2 hours*. This means that food that needs to be thawed before preparation should be placed in the refrigerator overnight to ensure safe thawing. When serving hot food, such as at a potluck or buffet-style gathering, it should be held at a warm temperature only for a maximum of 2 hours. Reheated food should be heated to at least 165°F (75°C) to ensure food safety.

Save some pasta water: To prevent pasta from absorbing too much sauce, reserve some of the pasta cooking water. After the pasta has absorbed some of the sauce, adding a small amount of the pasta cooking water can help loosen the sauce without diluting it. The pasta water contains starch from the pasta, which helps this process.

Opt for unsalted butter: Unsalted butter and salted butter have a few notable differences. Beyond the obvious disparity in salt content, it's important to recognize that different brands of salted butter may vary in the amount of salt used. By using unsalted butter, you control the level of salt in your recipe. Additionally, salted butter generally contains 10 to 18 percent more water than unsalted butter, which can impact the outcome of certain recipes.

Taste and season as you cook: Taste your food throughout the cooking process to adjust seasonings and flavors. Seasonings are a personal preference, so this is a great way to develop your taste buds. Balancing and adjusting flavors takes practice, so taste as you cook!

Use a scale for baking: You will get better results with baking when you weigh the dry ingredients. There can be a big difference in weight, depending on how you fill the measuring cup, and the wrong measurement can greatly affect the outcome. For example, not enough flour can make your cookies spread or prevent your muffins from having a beautiful dome.

Use a timer: Kitchen timers are essential for cooking and baking! Not setting a timer can result in either underbaking or overbaking your food. It's easy to get distracted in the kitchen, so a timer can be a good reminder to keep an eye on your food.

Let meat rest: Let meat rest after cooking to allow the juices to redistribute. This will keep your meat juicy and tender instead of dry and chewy.

Cook meat to the proper temperature: I often struggle to remember the right cooking temperatures for meat. So if you're anything like me, here is a quick guide to follow:

- BEEF:
  Rare: 130°F (55°C)
  Medium-rare: 135°F (58°C)
  Medium: 145°F (63°C)
  Medium-well: 155°F (69°C)
  Well: Over 160°F (71°C)

- CHICKEN:
  165–175°F (74–79°C)

- PORK:
  145°F (63°C)

BREAKFAST

I'm thrilled to share some of my family's beloved breakfast recipes in this section. Get ready to savor the goodness of my **Grandma's Homemade Pancakes** (page 28). Or if you're craving something savory, indulge in my mouthwatering **Avocado Toast with Fried Egg** (page 42), scrumptious **Homemade Biscuits and Gravy** (page 32), or delectable **Breakfast Enchiladas with Creamy Cheese Sauce** (page 44). And for those with a sweet tooth, don't miss the irresistible **Ooey Gooey Sticky Buns** (page 36) that are sure to make your mornings even sweeter.

◄ *My girls love to help me make breakfast in the kitchen on Saturday mornings. We make Grandma's Homemade Pancakes, and everyone loves adding their favorite toppings. Add a side of bacon, and it will bring even the teenagers from their rooms.*

EASY FRENCH TOAST

| SERVES 8 |

This breakfast favorite is requested all the time at our house. Thick bread is dipped in
a creamy mixture of milk, eggs, cinnamon, and vanilla extract and lightly fried. Top it with maple
syrup and berries of your choice, and every bite will taste like a little bit of heaven!

PREP TIME
5 minutes

COOK TIME
10 minutes

TOTAL TIME
15 minutes

4 eggs

⅔ cup 2% milk

1½ tsp ground cinnamon

1 tbsp vanilla extract

8 slices thick bread
(Texas toast or French bread)

2 tbsp unsalted butter

OPTIONAL TOPPINGS

Fresh berries

Confectioners' sugar

Maple syrup

1. In a medium bowl, whisk together the eggs and milk until smooth.
   Add the cinnamon and vanilla extract, and whisk to combine.

2. Fully submerge each slice of bread in the egg mixture.

3. Preheat a large skillet over medium heat. Add the butter. When the
   butter has melted and the pan is hot, add the soaked bread in batches.
   Fry for 2 minutes or until golden brown. Flip over and cook on the other
   side for 2 minutes.

4. Top with fresh berries, confectioners' sugar, and maple syrup, if using, or
   your favorite toppings, and serve.

To view on device

45-MINUTE CINNAMON ROLLS

| SERVES 9 |

Whoever said cinnamon rolls were meant to be a breakfast food only does not know my family. We love making these quick and easy cinnamon rolls, and we eat them for every occasion, no matter what time of day. Spread on the sweet glaze, and you will want to lick your fingers clean!

PREP TIME
25 minutes

COOK TIME
20 minutes

TOTAL TIME
45 minutes

2 ¾ cups all-purpose flour

¼ cup granulated sugar

¾ tsp salt

1 (0.25oz/7g) package instant yeast
   (or 2¼ tsp)

½ cup water

¼ cup 2% milk

2 tbsp unsalted butter

1 large egg

For the dough

1. To make the dough, in a large bowl, whisk together the all-purpose flour, granulated sugar, salt, and instant yeast. Set aside.

2. In a small bowl, combine the water, milk, and butter. Heat in the microwave for 30 to 45 seconds or until the butter is melted.

3. Using a fork, stir the melted butter liquid into the dry ingredients. Add the egg, and knead by hand or with a stand mixer for 5 or 6 minutes until the dough is no longer sticky. Form the dough into a ball, return to the bowl, cover, and let rest for 5 minutes.

½ cup packed brown sugar

2 tbsp ground cinnamon

¼ cup salted butter, softened

¼ cup heavy cream

For the filling

1. Preheat the oven to 200°F (95°C). Spray a 9×9-inch (23×23cm) pan with cooking spray.

2. In a small bowl, combine the brown sugar and cinnamon.

3. After the dough has rested, dust a clean surface lightly with more flour, and roll out the dough into a 15×9-inch (38×23cm) rectangle.

4. Spread the softened butter over the dough, and dust evenly with the cinnamon-sugar mixture. Tightly roll up the dough, and cut it into 9 even pieces. Place the rolls in the prepared pan, and cover with plastic wrap or foil.

5. Turn off the warmed oven, place the pan of rolls inside, and let them rise for 20 minutes. After 20 minutes, uncover and drizzle the heavy cream evenly over the top of the rolls.

6. Return the rolls to the oven, and heat the oven to 375°F (190°C). Bake for 15 to 20 minutes or until the tops of the rolls are golden brown.

To view on device

4oz (115g) cream cheese, at room temperature

1 cup confectioners' sugar

1 tsp vanilla extract

2–3 tbsp 2% milk

For the cream cheese glaze

1. In a medium bowl, and using a mixer on medium, beat the cream cheese, confectioners' sugar, vanilla extract, and 2 tablespoons milk until smooth. Add more milk as needed.

2. Let the rolls cool for 20 minutes or so before spreading the glaze over the top. Serve warm. Store any leftovers at room temperature for up to 4 days. You can reheat them in the microwave on high for 20 to 30 seconds.

Pan Cakes for 4

1 C. flour
1/4 teas salt
2 tlbs sugar
2 tlbs baking powder

1 egg (beaten)
2 tbbs oil
(or melted shortening
1 cup milk

Mix egg, oil + milk in bowl. Add dry ingredients that have been mixed together. Fry

GRANDMA'S HOMEMADE PANCAKES

| SERVES 4 |

My grandma and I share a love for food, and some of the best tried and true recipes come from her, including her from-scratch pancakes. These pancakes turn out so fluffy and perfect every single time. Drizzle on some sweet, warm syrup or top them with fresh berries, you won't be able to resist. These are a tradition at our house, and we make them every chance we get.

PREP TIME
5 minutes

COOK TIME
15 minutes

TOTAL TIME
20 minutes

1 egg
2 tbsp canola oil
1 cup 2% milk
1 cup all-purpose flour
¼ tsp salt
2 tbsp granulated sugar
2 tbsp baking powder

To view on device

1. Spray a large skillet with cooking spray, and preheat over medium heat.

2. In a medium bowl, whisk together the egg, canola oil, and milk.

3. In a separate medium bowl, combine the all-purpose flour, salt, sugar, and baking powder.

4. Add the dry ingredients to the wet ingredients, and stir to combine.

5. Drop about ⅓ cup of the batter onto the warm skillet. When bubbles form in the top of the pancake, flip it over and cook the other side until golden brown. Transfer the cooked pancake to a plate, cover with a towel to keep warm, and repeat with the remaining batter.

REFRESHING PEACH SMOOTHIE

| SERVES 2 |

There isn't anything much better than a deliciously creamy smoothie to start your day. This smoothie is full of peaches (I use frozen so I can make it all year long), bananas, and a burst of apple juice. As the flavors blend together, you are greeted with a cold and refreshing smoothie packed with all the fruit you need for the day!

PREP TIME	COOK TIME	TOTAL TIME
10 minutes	*None*	*10 minutes*

1. To a blender, add the ice, frozen peaches, frozen banana, apple juice, Greek yogurt, and honey.

2. Blend until smooth, and serve immediately.

NOTE

You can use fresh peaches in this recipe, but the consistency won't be quite as thick. I like to use frozen peaches because they add to the smoothie's icy texture and keep it thick and creamy.

1 cup ice cubes

2 cups frozen sliced peaches

1 frozen banana

1 cup apple juice, or peach juice

¼ cup Greek yogurt

2 tbsp honey

To view on device

AMAGING MIGAS
with Chorizo

| SERVES 5 |

This migas recipe is a delicious way to eat your veggies. Filled with flavor, the chorizo brings in a delicious taste that complements the veggies and fills you up.

PREP TIME
10 minutes

COOK TIME
20 minutes

TOTAL TIME
30 minutes

3 tbsp vegetable oil

4 corn tortillas, cut into 1-in (2.5cm) strips

1 small white onion, diced

1 green bell pepper, ribs and seeds removed, and diced

1 jalapeño, minced

3 cloves garlic, minced

½ lb (225g) chorizo

8 large eggs

2 tsp chili powder

1 tsp salt

¼ tsp freshly ground black pepper

1 cup shredded Monterey Jack cheese

¼ cup chopped fresh cilantro

OPTIONAL TOPPINGS

1 Roma tomato, diced

1 avocado, pitted and sliced

½ cup cotija cheese

1. In a medium skillet over medium-high heat, heat the vegetable oil. Add the tortilla strips, and fry for 2 or 3 minutes or until crispy. Set aside on a paper towel–lined plate.

2. Add the white onion, green bell pepper, and jalapeño to the skillet, and sauté for 3 or 4 minutes or until almost tender.

3. Add the garlic and chorizo, and cook, crumbling the chorizo, for 3 or 4 minutes or until no longer pink.

4. In a medium bowl, combine the eggs, chili powder, salt, and black pepper. Pour the mixture into the skillet with the chorizo, and cook for about 3 minutes or until the eggs are almost done.

5. Add the Monterey Jack cheese, cilantro, and tortilla strips, and continue to cook for 2 or 3 minutes or until the cheese has melted and the eggs are done.

6. Top with Roma tomatoes, avocado slices, and cotija cheese, if using, and serve.

HOMEMADE BISCUITS AND GRAVY

| SERVES 6 |

This is comfort food at its finest. The buttery biscuits have a perfect, flaky texture, and when you scoop on some of the rich and creamy sausage gravy ... well, you'll definitely want more. This classic meal is the perfect breakfast option all year long.

PREP TIME
30 minutes

COOK TIME
30 minutes

TOTAL TIME
1 hour

2 ¼ cups all-purpose flour

1 ½ tbsp baking powder

1 tsp salt

½ cup unsalted butter, cold

1 cup buttermilk

2 tbsp unsalted butter, melted, for brushing

For the biscuits

1. Preheat the oven to 425°F (220°C). Line a baking sheet with parchment paper.

2. In a large bowl, whisk together the all-purpose flour, baking powder, and salt.

3. Using a cheese grater, grate the cold butter into the flour mixture. Use a pastry cutter or the back of a fork to cut the butter into the flour mixture.

4. After the butter is incorporated, add the buttermilk. Use a pastry cutter or fork to mix the buttermilk into the dough. Stop mixing just before it all comes together. The dough should be shaggy and crumbly at this point.

5. Turn out the dough onto a floured surface, and knead with your hands to bring it together. Be careful not to overwork the dough or handle it too much because you want the butter to stay as cold as possible.

6. Roll out the dough on the floured surface until it's 1 inch (2.5cm) thick. Using a 3-inch (7.5cm) biscuit cutter or cup, cut the biscuits. Gather the dough scraps, form them into a ball, roll out the dough again, and repeat the cutting process until all the dough has been used. You should have 6 biscuits.

7. Place the biscuits 1 inch (2.5cm) apart on the prepared baking sheet, and brush melted butter on top of each biscuit.

8. Bake for 15 to 20 minutes or until lightly golden brown on top and bottom.

9. Transfer the biscuits to a rack to cool while you prepare the gravy.

To view on device

1 lb (450g) ground breakfast sausage

⅓ cup all-purpose flour

½ tsp kosher salt

½ tsp freshly ground black pepper

¼ tsp **Easy Italian Seasoning**
(page 263, optional)

2 ¾ cups half-and-half

2 tbsp unsalted butter

For the gravy

1. In a large nonstick skillet over medium heat, cook the breakfast sausage for about 5 minutes or until lightly browned and no longer pink.

2. Sprinkle the all-purpose flour, kosher salt, black pepper, and Easy Italian Seasoning, if using, over the cooked sausage. Stir and cook for about 1 minute or until the flour is absorbed.

3. Slowly whisk in the half-and-half. Increase the heat to medium-high, and bring to a boil.

4. Reduce the heat to a rapid simmer, and cook, stirring occasionally, for about 5 minutes or until the sauce is thickened and coats the back of a spoon. If the sauce is too thick, you can add more half-and-half or milk, 1 tablespoon at a time, until it reaches the desired consistency.

5. Whisk the butter into the gravy. (This gives it a rich, velvety finish.) Taste, and season with more salt and pepper if needed.

6. Split the biscuits in half, and serve the sausage gravy over the top.

THE PERFECT CREPES

| SERVES 12 |

My husband lived in France for two years and developed a love for crepes. Our family begs for this recipe, and we cook it often. My favorite part is changing out the toppings. You can use fruit and confectioners' sugar, or you can try jams, chocolate-hazelnut or other spreads, or really, any flavors you love!

PREP TIME	COOK TIME	TOTAL TIME
5 minutes	*20 minutes*	*25 minutes*

2 cups all-purpose flour

2 ¼ cups 2% milk

¼ cup granulated sugar

4 large eggs

¼ cup unsalted butter, melted

1 tsp vanilla extract

Olive oil, for brushing

8oz (225g) cream cheese

2 ½ tbsp confectioners' sugar, plus more for topping (optional)

8oz (225g) whipped topping

Sliced fruit, for topping (optional)

1. In a blender, pulse together the all-purpose flour, milk, granulated sugar, eggs, butter, and vanilla extract until the batter is completely smooth.

2. Brush a medium pan with olive oil, and set over medium heat. When hot, add about ¼ to ½ cup batter. Swirl the pan in a circular motion to spread the batter into a thin and even circle. (A crepe spatula is helpful here if you have one.)

3. Heat on one side for 30 to 40 seconds and then flip over. The cooked side will start to dry out, and tiny bubbles will form. Transfer the cooked crepe to a plate, cover with a towel to keep warm, and repeat with the rest of the batter.

4. In a medium bowl, beat together the cream cheese and confectioners' sugar until smooth. Fold in the whipped topping.

5. Spoon 2 tablespoons cream cheese filling onto each crepe, and fold or roll up the crepe.

6. Top with sliced fresh fruit, dust with additional confectioners' sugar, if using, and serve.

To view on device

OOEY GOOEY STICKY BUNS

| SERVES 10 |

This sticky bun recipe has been a holiday tradition in our family for years.
It was introduced to us by my boys' grandma, and we have been hooked
ever since. They are warm and gooey—not to mention so easy to make!

PREP TIME
5 minutes + overnight to rise

COOK TIME
25 minutes

TOTAL TIME
30 minutes + overnight

½ cup chopped pecans or walnuts
(optional)

20 frozen dinner rolls
(Rhodes brand recommended)

1 (3.5oz/100g) package butterscotch
pudding (not instant)

1 tsp ground cinnamon

½ cup unsalted butter, melted

½ cup packed brown sugar

1. Lightly coat a Bundt pan with cooking spray. Add chopped pecans or walnuts, if using, to the bottom of the pan. Place the dinner rolls in the pan on top of the nuts.

2. Sprinkle the butterscotch pudding powder over the rolls, followed by the cinnamon.

3. In a small bowl, combine the melted butter and brown sugar. Drizzle over the rolls.

4. Cover the pan with a damp cloth, and allow to rise overnight at room temperature.

5. Preheat the oven to 350°F (175°C) and bake for 25 minutes. After about 10 minutes, cover the pan with foil and continue to bake. (The top browns fast, and the foil helps the rolls cook throughout and not brown quite as quickly. But do cook for the whole time or else the rolls on the bottom will be doughy.) Remove from the oven, and let sit for 2 or 3 minutes.

6. Invert a plate on top of the Bundt pan, and carefully flip over to transfer the sticky buns to the plate. Scrape out any leftover glaze and nuts from the pan, and add them to the top of the sticky buns. Serve warm.

NOTE

This recipe can be made in a 9×13-inch (23×33cm) baking pan if you don't have a Bundt pan. Lightly coat the pan with cooking spray, and place the nuts in the bottom. Add the rolls in a single layer over the nuts, and pour the pudding, cinnamon, and butter mixture on top. Cover with a damp cloth, and allow to rise overnight at room temperature. Bake uncovered at 350°F (175°C) for 25 minutes.

To view on device

LOADED VEGGIE FRITTATA
with Smoked Gouda

COOKBOOK EXCLUSIVE

| SERVES 6 |

This delicious baked egg dish is loaded with veggies and smoked gouda. Frittatas are often served at room temperature, making them the perfect dish to serve at brunch or for a crowd when you don't have to worry about serving something hot. Impress your guests with this yummy meal to start their day!

PREP TIME	COOK TIME	TOTAL TIME
10 minutes	*15 minutes*	*25 minutes*

1. Preheat the oven to 375°F (190°C).

2. In a medium bowl, combine the eggs, heavy cream, smoked gouda cheese, kosher salt, and black pepper. Set aside.

3. In a 9-inch (23cm) cast-iron pan or oven-safe skillet over medium-high heat, heat the olive oil. Add the red onion, broccoli, zucchini, and red bell pepper, and sauté for 3 minutes.

4. Add the baby spinach, and cook for 2 or 3 minutes or until it wilts.

5. Stir in the cherry tomatoes and green onions, and pour the egg mixture over the vegetables.

6. Bake for 15 to 20 minutes or until the top is golden brown and the egg mixture is set. Allow to come to room temperature, and serve.

10 eggs

½ cup heavy cream

1 cup shredded smoked gouda cheese

1 tsp kosher salt

½ tsp freshly ground black pepper

2 tbsp olive oil

¼ cup chopped red onion

1 cup chopped broccoli florets

½ cup chopped zucchini

⅓ cup chopped red bell pepper

2 cups baby spinach

½ cup cherry tomatoes, halved

3 tbsp sliced green onions

THE BEST BREAKFAST CASSEROLE

| SERVES 12 |

I love a good breakfast casserole. This hearty and flavorful egg-and-cheese blend
is perfect for any morning. I love that I can prepare this ahead of time and bake
it fresh, just before I need to serve it. It makes a perfect breakfast for holidays.

PREP TIME
5 minutes + 2 hours to refrigerate

COOK TIME
1 hour 30 minutes

TOTAL TIME
3 hours 35 minutes

24oz (680g) frozen shredded potatoes

Salt and freshly ground black pepper

12 large eggs

2 cups half-and-half

1 tsp seasoning salt

1½ cups grated cheddar cheese

1½ cups grated pepper jack cheese

2 cups chopped ham, or cooked
sausage

Sliced green onions, for garnish

1. Lightly coat a 9×13-inch (23×33cm) baking pan with cooking spray.
   Add the frozen shredded potatoes to the bottom of the pan, and sprinkle
   with salt and black pepper.

2. In a large bowl, whisk together the eggs. Add the half-and-half,
   seasoning salt, cheddar cheese, pepper jack cheese, and ham.

3. Pour the egg mixture over the frozen potatoes. Cover with foil, and
   refrigerate for 2 hours or overnight.

4. Preheat the oven to 350°F (175°C) and bake uncovered for 90 minutes.
   Let rest for 10 minutes, then garnish with green onions and serve.

To view on device

OVEN-BAKED GERMAN PANCAKE

| SERVES 4 |

This classic breakfast is always a huge hit at our house, and it will become a favorite at your home, too. Cooked right in the skillet, this golden, puffy pancake is so easy to make. Topped with some fruit and confectioners' sugar, this breakfast is great for special occasions or holidays all throughout the year.

PREP TIME
5 minutes

COOK TIME
20 minutes

TOTAL TIME
25 minutes

3 large eggs

½ cup 2% milk

3 tbsp unsalted butter, melted

1 tbsp granulated sugar

¼ tsp salt

½ cup all-purpose flour

1. Preheat the oven to 450°F (230°C).

2. In a medium bowl, whisk the eggs, milk, 2 tablespoons melted butter, sugar, and salt. Add the all-purpose flour, and stir until incorporated. Be careful not to overmix.

3. Add the remaining 1 tablespoon melted butter to the bottom of a 9- or 11-inch (23 or 28cm) cast-iron skillet. Pour the batter into the skillet, and bake for 12 to 18 minutes or until the edges start to brown. Top with your desired toppings, and serve.

To view on device

COOKBOOK EXCLUSIVE

AVOCADO TOAST
with Fried Egg

| SERVES 4 |

This avocado toast is a savory breakfast that fills you up. The mashed avocado is full of flavor, and when you add it to toasted bread and top it with a fried egg, you have a healthy, hearty breakfast. Packed with protein and healthy fats, this classic breakfast will become a go-to.

PREP TIME
5 minutes

COOK TIME
5 minutes

TOTAL TIME
10 minutes

2 tsp olive oil or unsalted butter

4 large eggs

2 ripe avocados, pitted

1 tbsp freshly squeezed lemon juice

2 tbsp chopped red onion

½ tsp garlic powder

Salt and freshly ground black pepper

4 slices bread, toasted

Sesame seeds, for garnish

1. In a large nonstick skillet over low heat, heat the olive oil or butter for about 3 minutes.

2. Crack the first egg, and slowly add it to one side of the skillet. You should **not** hear a sizzle when it hits the pan. If you do hear a sizzle, your skillet is too hot, so reduce the heat a little. Repeat with the remaining eggs, adding each to a separate "corner" of the skillet. Cover with a tight lid, and cook for 2 to 2½ minutes or until the whites are completely set but the yolks are still runny. Watch it closely, but don't remove the lid until after 2 minutes.

3. In a medium bowl, mash the avocados with a fork to the desired consistency. Add the lemon juice, red onion, garlic powder, and salt and black pepper, and mix well.

4. Spread ¼ of the avocado mixture onto each slice of toasted bread. Top each with 1 fried egg, garnish with sesame seeds, and serve.

MORNING GLORY MUFFINS

| SERVES 14 |

Packed with nutrients, these hearty muffins are the perfect way to start your day. With filling ingredients like flaxseeds, coconut, carrots, and sunflower seeds, this flavorful muffin will keep you satisfied until lunch.

PREP TIME	COOK TIME	TOTAL TIME
20 minutes	*25 minutes*	*45 minutes*

2 cups whole-wheat flour

1 cup packed dark brown sugar

1½ tsp baking soda

2 tsp ground cinnamon

½ tsp ground ginger

½ tsp salt

¼ cup ground flaxseeds

1 cup shredded skin-on tart apple

2 cups shredded carrots

⅓ cup shredded coconut

½ cup raisins

½ cup chopped walnuts

¼ cup sunflower seeds

3 large eggs

½ cup vegetable oil

¼ cup pineapple juice

1. Preheat the oven to 400°F (205°C). Line a muffin pan with paper liners, and lightly coat the liners with cooking spray. (This recipe makes 14 or 15 muffins, so either prep a second pan or bake the muffins in batches.)

2. In a large bowl, whisk together the whole-wheat flour, dark brown sugar, baking soda, cinnamon, ginger, salt, and flaxseeds.

3. Add the apple, carrots, coconut, raisins, walnuts, and sunflower seeds, and stir to combine.

4. In a medium bowl, combine the eggs, vegetable oil, and pineapple juice.

5. Add the wet ingredients to the dry, and mix until combined.

6. Scoop the batter into the prepared muffin liners, filling them completely.

7. Bake for 5 minutes and then reduce the oven temperature to 350°F (175°C) and bake for 16 to 18 more minutes or until a toothpick comes out clean. Store any leftovers in an airtight container at room temperature for up to 4 days.

NOTE

These muffins freeze well. After the muffins have cooled, seal them in an airtight container and place in the freezer, where they'll keep for 3 months. Thaw at room temperature overnight.

To view on device

BREAKFAST ENCHILADAS
with Creamy Cheese Sauce

| SERVES 10 |

I absolutely love a hearty breakfast, which is why breakfast enchiladas are a favorite at our house. These enchiladas pack a punch with a cheesy, green chile sauce. The sausage, salsa, and egg flavors combine for a delicious breakfast option.

PREP TIME
15 minutes

COOK TIME
40 minutes

TOTAL TIME
55 minutes

FOR THE GREEN CHILE CHEESE SAUCE

¼ cup salted butter

¼ cup all-purpose flour

2 cups 2% milk

1 (4.5oz/125g) can chopped green chiles

2 cups shredded sharp cheddar cheese

FOR THE ENCHILADA FILLING

1 lb (450g) ground sausage

½ cup salsa

10 large eggs, beaten

½ tsp salt

¼ tsp freshly ground black pepper

½ tsp onion powder

1–2 tbsp water

10 flour tortillas

2 cups shredded Mexican or Monterey Jack cheese

OPTIONAL TOPPINGS

Chopped avocado

Diced Roma tomatoes

Chopped green onions

Chopped fresh cilantro

1. To make the green chile cheese sauce, in a medium saucepan over medium-high heat, melt the butter. Whisk in the all-purpose flour, and slowly whisk in the milk. Add the green chiles and shredded sharp cheddar cheese, and cook, whisking, until the cheese is melted.

2. Preheat the oven to 375°F (190°C). Lightly coat a 9×13-inch (23×33cm) baking dish with cooking spray.

3. In a large saucepan over medium-high heat, cook the sausage for 5 to 7 minutes or until fully cooked. Drain the oil from the pan and discard. Add salsa to the meat, and stir to combine. Remove the sausage mixture from the pan, and set it aside.

4. In a medium bowl, whisk together the eggs, salt, black pepper, and onion powder. Add 1 or 2 tablespoons water to the mixture to help make your eggs fluffy.

5. Add the eggs to the large saucepan, and cook over medium heat for 5 or 6 minutes or until the eggs are scrambled. Add the cooked sausage mixture to the eggs, and stir until combined.

6. Fill each tortilla with about a ½ cup sausage and egg mixture. Sprinkle a small amount of shredded Mexican or Monterey Jack cheese over the filling, and roll the tortilla tightly around the filling. Place the rolled tortilla in the prepared baking dish, seam side down. Repeat with the remaining tortillas and filling until the baking dish is full. (You may have filling left over, depending on how full you fill the tortillas.) Pour the green chile cheese sauce evenly over the enchiladas, and top with the remaining shredded cheese.

7. Bake for 20 to 25 minutes or until the cheese is melted.

8. Top the enchiladas with chopped avocado, diced Roma tomatoes, chopped green onions, chopped cilantro, if using, or your desired toppings, and serve.

BREADS

When I want to fill my home with a delicious, comforting scent, I bake bread. My grandma taught me her special bread recipe (**Grandma's Homemade Bread**, page 54), and I still remember eagerly waiting for that warm, buttery slice straight from the oven. My kids love helping me make **Easy Homemade Garlic Knots** (page 55), but if you prefer something sweet, try our **Family Favorite Banana Bread** (page 49).

◀ *I will take freshly baked bread over sweets any day of the week! Nothing beats a warm slice of homemade bread slathered with some butter and jam!*

FAMILY FAVORITE BANANA BREAD

| SERVES 10 |

This banana bread is a delightful treat. Made with mashed ripe bananas,
it has a natural sweetness that is perfectly complemented by the nutty crunch of
walnuts. Each loaf is soft, tender, and bursting with banana flavor in every bite.

PREP TIME
15 minutes

COOK TIME
35 minutes

TOTAL TIME
50 minutes

3 ripe bananas, mashed (about 1 cup)

1 tsp baking soda

½ cup vegetable oil

⅔ cup granulated sugar

2 large eggs, beaten

Pinch of salt

1⅓ cups all-purpose flour

½ cup chopped walnuts (optional)

1. Preheat the oven to 350°F (175°C). Lightly coat a 9×5-inch (23×12.5cm) loaf pan with cooking spray.

2. In a large bowl, and using a spatula or wooden spoon, mix together the bananas, baking soda, vegetable oil, sugar, eggs, salt, and all-purpose flour. Fold in the chopped walnuts, if using.

3. Pour the batter into the prepared loaf pan, and bake for 35 to 40 minutes or until a toothpick comes out clean.

4. Let the bread cool in the pan for 5 minutes and then transfer to a wire rack to finish cooling. Store any leftovers in an airtight container at room temperature for up to 4 days.

NOTE

For strawberry banana bread, omit the walnuts, combine 1 cup chopped fresh strawberries with 1 tablespoon all-purpose flour, and fold the coated strawberries into the finished batter just before baking.

To view on device

ROSEMARY PARMESAN BREAD

| SERVES 6–8 |

Any time I get a chance, I love to experiment with baking different loaves of bread that are filled with unique flavors. This bread really knocks it out of the park with its fresh taste and delicious crust. I love topping it with Parmesan cheese to really bring together the flavors.

PREP TIME	COOK TIME	TOTAL TIME
2 hours 30 minutes	*50 minutes*	*3 hours 20 minutes*

1½ cups warm water

1 (0.25oz/7g) package active dry yeast (or 2¼ tsp)

1 tsp granulated sugar

¼ cup olive oil

1½ tsp salt

2 ½–3 cups all-purpose flour

2 tbsp chopped fresh rosemary, plus more for garnish

1¼ cups grated Parmesan cheese (freshly grated preferred), plus more for garnish

1. In a small bowl, combine the warm water, active dry yeast, and granulated sugar. Let sit for about 5 minutes or until the yeast becomes foamy.

2. In the bowl of a stand mixer fitted with the paddle, or in a large bowl and using a handheld mixer with a dough hook, combine the yeast mixture, olive oil, salt, and 2½ cups all-purpose flour. (If you don't have a stand mixer or dough hook, you can knead the dough thoroughly by hand.)

3. Begin mixing on low, adding more flour ¼ cup at a time if needed, until all the flour is incorporated. Add just enough flour to bring together the dough. (This is a fairly wet dough.)

4. When the dough has come together, add the rosemary and Parmesan cheese, and mix for 2 minutes on medium. This helps develop the gluten.

5. Remove the dough from the mixer bowl, and place it in a large bowl greased with olive oil. Cover with plastic wrap, and let the dough sit for about 1 hour or until it has doubled in size.

6. Turn out the dough onto a floured surface and punch down, or degas, it. Knead the dough for a few minutes to further build the gluten structure. Return the dough to the oiled bowl, cover it with plastic wrap, and allow it to rest for 30 minutes.

7. Turn out the dough onto a lightly floured surface, and degas it. Work the dough into a tight ball, but not so tight that the skin tears. Line the oiled bowl with parchment paper, and place the ball back in the bowl, seam side down. Let it rest for about 30 minutes or until it has just about doubled in size.

8. Meanwhile, prepare an enamel-coated Dutch oven by placing it in the oven and preheating it to 425°F (220°C). When the dough is ready to bake, remove the Dutch oven from the preheated oven.

9. Carefully transfer the dough and parchment paper to the heated Dutch oven. Using a paring knife, score the top of the loaf and then sprinkle

more Parmesan cheese and rosemary over the top. Cover the Dutch oven with the lid, return it to the oven, and bake for 30 minutes.

10. After 30 minutes, remove the lid. Continue baking uncovered for 15 to 20 minutes. The loaf is ready when it is golden brown on the surface and the internal temperature reaches 190°F (90°C).

11. Remove the loaf from the Dutch oven and allow to cool for at least 30 minutes before slicing and serving.

NOTE

To achieve a light sourdough flavor, leave the dough in the refrigerator overnight or for up to 2 days. I gave my dough two folds, each a half an hour apart, and covered the bowl with plastic wrap. After the first 24 hours, I gave it another fold and returned it to the refrigerator. On the last day, I did the final form and let it proof at room temperature.

JALAPEÑO CHEDDAR BREAD

| SERVES 6–8 |

This bread is the perfect combination of heat and cheesiness—
the jalapeños add quite a kick, and the cheddar brings rich flavor. The bread
is delicious on its own or easily complements any sandwich or soup.

PREP TIME
20 minutes + 90 minutes to rise

COOK TIME
50 minutes

TOTAL TIME
2 hours 40 minutes

1 (0.25oz/7g) packet instant yeast
(2¼ tsp)

1½ cups warm water

1 tbsp honey

3–4 cups bread flour

1 tbsp salt

⅔ cup sliced pickled jalapeños,
plus more for topping

2 cups shredded cheddar cheese,
plus more for topping

NOTE

The temperature of the area where the dough is left to rest affects how quickly it rises. Warmer temperatures make the dough proof quicker; cooler temperatures slow it down. Likewise, the temperature of the liquids you add will affect the dough. Adjust for these variables as you can. Also, this is a fairly spicy bread. If you prefer a milder flavor, you can reduce the amount of jalapeños used.

1. In a large bowl, combine the instant yeast, warm water, and honey. Let the yeast proof for about 5 minutes or until frothy.

2. Add 3 cups bread flour, salt, jalapeños, and cheddar cheese. Using a mixer fitted with a dough hook on low, blend for about 5 minutes or until all the ingredients come together. The dough shouldn't be too sticky and should come clean from the bowl easily. If you need to add more flour, do so in ¼-cup increments.

3. Increase the speed to medium-high, and mix for 3 to 5 minutes. This builds and strengthens the gluten in the dough. Transfer the dough to a lightly oiled bowl, and turn the dough a few times so it is evenly coated with the oil. Cover the bowl with a towel or plastic wrap, and let rest for 45 minutes to 1 hour or until doubled in size.

4. Turn out the dough onto a lightly floured surface, and degas. Fold and work the dough into a tight ball but not so tight that the skin tears. Line the oiled bowl with parchment paper, and place the dough in the bowl. Cover the bowl with a towel, and let the dough rest for about 30 minutes or until just about doubled.

5. Meanwhile, prepare an enamel-coated Dutch oven by placing it in the oven and preheating it to 425°F (220°C). When the dough is ready to bake, remove the Dutch oven from the heated oven and carefully transfer the dough and parchment paper to the Dutch oven. Score the top of the loaf, and sprinkle with cheese and jalapeños. Cover the Dutch oven with the lid, return it to the oven, and bake for 30 minutes.

6. After 30 minutes, remove the lid. Bake, uncovered, for 15 to 20 minutes more or until the loaf is golden brown and the internal temperature reaches 190°F (90°C). Remove the loaf from the Dutch oven, and cool for at least 30 minutes before slicing and serving. Store any leftovers in an airtight container at room temperature for up to 1 week.

GRANDMA'S HOMEMADE BREAD

| SERVES 16 |

The first time I made bread I was with my grandma. Sitting on a stool, she walked me through each step of preparing the bread. When it was done, she let us kids have a warm slice, fresh from the oven, covered with butter. The house smelled so delicious. To this day, I can't smell this bread without thinking of my grandma.

PREP TIME	COOK TIME	TOTAL TIME
15 minutes + 3 hours to rise	35 minutes	3 hours 50 minutes

2 ½ cups warm water

¼ cup granulated sugar

1 ¼ tsp salt

1 tbsp active dry yeast

5 cups all-purpose flour

2 tbsp olive oil

1. In a large bowl, combine the warm water, sugar, salt, and active dry yeast. Let the yeast proof for about 5 minutes or until frothy. Using a mixer fitted with a dough hook on low, add the all-purpose flour 1 cup at a time and mix until the ingredients combine to form a soft dough.

2. Turn out the dough onto a floured surface, and knead until smooth and elastic. Form the dough into a ball.

3. Add the olive oil to the bowl. Return the dough to the bowl, and turn the dough a few times so it is evenly coated with the oil. Cover with a towel, and let it rise for 1 to 1½ hours or until doubled in size.

4. Lightly coat two 9×5-inch (23×12.5cm) baking pans with cooking spray, and dust with flour.

5. Turn out the dough onto a flat surface, and degas. Cut the dough in half, roll each half, and place the loaves into the prepared baking pans. Let the loaves rise for another 1 to 1½ hours or until doubled.

6. Preheat the oven to 350°F (175°C). Bake for 30 to 35 minutes or until the loaf is golden brown on top. Let cool for 10 minutes before removing from the pan, slicing, and serving. Store any leftovers in an airtight container at room temperature for up to 1 week.

To view on device

1½ cups warm water

2 tbsp granulated sugar

1 tbsp active dry yeast

3½ cups all-purpose flour, plus more
   for dusting

1 tbsp salt

½ cup unsalted butter

1 tbsp garlic powder

1 tsp minced fresh parsley

1 tsp olive oil

¼ cup grated Parmesan cheese

EASY HOMEMADE GARLIC KNOTS

| SERVES 8 |

These tasty garlic knots complement any entrée. Buttery and warm, they bake in less than 20 minutes, making them the perfect option for any meal.

PREP TIME	COOK TIME	TOTAL TIME
25 minutes	*15 minutes*	*40 minutes*

1. In a large bowl, mix together the warm water, sugar and active dry yeast. Set aside for 5 minutes.

2. To the yeast mixture, add the all-purpose flour and salt. Using a mixer with a dough hook attachment on medium, mix until smooth. Remove the dough hook, and let the dough rise for 10 minutes.

3. Preheat the oven to 400°F (205°C). Lightly coat a baking sheet with cooking spray, and lightly flour your work surface.

4. Turn out the dough onto the prepared work surface, and roll it to about ½ inch (1.25cm) thick. Using a pizza cutter, cut the dough in half and then into eight 8- to 10-inch (20–25.5cm) strips. Roll the strips between your hands until they're like ropes and then loosely tie into knots. Place the knots 2 inches (5cm) apart on the prepared baking sheet and allow to rise for 10 more minutes.

5. After 10 minutes, transfer to the oven, and bake for 15 to 20 minutes.

6. Meanwhile, melt the butter and mix it with the garlic powder, parsley, and olive oil.

7. When the garlic knots come out of the oven, brush the tops with the butter-garlic mixture, sprinkle with Parmesan cheese, and serve.

To view on device

1-HOUR DINNER ROLLS

| SERVES 15 |

These dinner rolls come together so quickly, and they turn out perfectly
soft, every single time. This will become your new go-to roll recipe!

PREP TIME
*15 minutes + 30 minutes to rest
and rise*

COOK TIME
18 minutes

TOTAL TIME
1 hour 3 minutes

3 ½ cups all-purpose flour

3 tbsp granulated sugar

1 tbsp instant yeast

1½ tsp salt

1¼ cups warm 1% milk

6 tbsp melted unsalted butter, divided

1. Preheat the oven to warm or the lowest temperature possible, about
   170°F (77°C). Lightly coat a 9×13-inch (23×33cm) baking pan with
   cooking spray.

2. In a large bowl, whisk together the all-purpose flour, sugar, instant yeast,
   and salt.

3. In a medium bowl, combine the warm milk and 4 tablespoons melted
   butter. Slowly add the liquid to the dry ingredients, and use a mixer
   fitted with a dough hook on low to knead the dough for about 4 minutes
   or until it's smooth and elastic. If the dough is still very sticky, add more
   flour, 1 or 2 tablespoons at a time.

4. When the dough is smooth, cover the bowl with a towel and let the dough
   rest for 5 to 10 minutes.

5. Turn out the rested dough onto a lightly floured surface, and evenly
   divide it into 15 pieces. (You can use a kitchen scale to weigh the whole
   dough ball and divide that by 15 to get the weight of each roll.) Shape
   each piece into a ball, and pinch the dough together on the bottom.

6. Place the dough balls in the prepared baking pan, and use your fingers
   to rub a little water over the tops so they don't dry out while baking.
   Transfer the pan of rolls to the warm oven to rise for 20 minutes or up to
   30 minutes if the rolls haven't doubled in size after 20. (It helps to mist
   the bottom of the oven with a spray bottle to create steam to help the
   rolls rise faster.)

7. Remove the risen rolls from the oven, and increase the heat to 375°F
   (190°C).

8. Return the rolls to the oven and bake for 16 to 18 minutes or until the
   tops are golden brown. Brush with the remaining 2 tablespoons melted
   butter as soon as they come out of the oven, and serve warm. Store any
   leftovers in an airtight container at room temperature for up to 4 days.

To view on device

LUNCH

Finding the perfect lunch option always has been a challenge for me. It's not easy to strike a balance between something filling, healthy, and suitable for just one person or an entire family. To simplify things for you, I've compiled a collection of my favorite lunch recipes that cater to those on the go as well as families looking for something new to try. If you're flying solo, I recommend my delectable **Chicken Salad** (page 60). It's a satisfying and nutritious choice that will keep you going throughout the day. If you're serving a hungry household, my **Ultimate Tuna Melt** (page 74) or **Chicken Parmesan Sandwiches** (page 78) are guaranteed crowd-pleasers. For those with kids, the **Easy French Dip Sliders** (page 63) or the **Crispy Parmesan Air-Fryer Chicken Tenders** (page 79) are absolute winners. These recipes are not only delicious but also kid-friendly, ensuring that everyone at the table will be satisfied.

◄ *I could eat this chicken salad for lunch literally every single day. And not to toot my own horn, but it is the best recipe I have ever had!*

CHICKEN SALAD

| SERVES 8 |

This recipe is a must for any occasion and the perfect choice to feed a crowd.
The combined flavors of chicken, veggies, and grapes, and the added crunch of pecans,
will make you want to have seconds. This chicken salad can't be missed!

PREP TIME
15 minutes

COOK TIME
None

TOTAL TIME
15 minutes

2 ½ cups cooked and shredded chicken

1 cup halved seedless red grapes

1 cup chopped pecans

4 green onions, chopped

½ cup finely diced celery

1 cup mayonnaise or Greek yogurt

Juice of ½ lemon (about 1 ½ tbsp)

1 tbsp Dijon mustard

Salt and freshly ground black pepper

1. In a medium bowl, combine the chicken, grapes, pecans, green onions, celery, mayonnaise, lemon juice, and Dijon mustard. Season with salt and black pepper.

2. Serve with croissants, romaine, or crackers. Store any leftovers in an airtight container in the refrigerator for up to 4 days.

To view on device

EASY FRENCH DIP SLIDERS

| SERVES 4 |

I love an easy meal, and these sliders, filled with tender roast beef and melted provolone cheese, are perfect for an entrée, lunch, or an appetizer. They can be eaten plain or dipped in some au jus sauce. Either way, your family will love them.

PREP TIME
10 minutes

COOK TIME
30 minutes

TOTAL TIME
40 minutes

4 tbsp unsalted butter, melted

1 (12-roll) package Hawaiian sweet rolls

6 slices provolone cheese

1 lb (450g) deli roast beef, or leftover sliced roast beef

¼ tsp garlic powder

1 tbsp dried onion flakes

1 (1oz/30g) package au jus sauce mix (about 2 ½ tbsp)

1. Preheat the oven to 350°F (175°C). Pour 2 tablespoons of the melted butter into the bottom of a 9×13-inch (23×33cm) baking dish, and swirl to coat.

2. Carefully remove the entire block of Hawaiian sweet rolls from the bag. Keeping the rolls together, use a serrated knife to slice all 12 rolls in half, at once, so you have a top and bottom piece.

3. Place the bottom piece of rolls in the baking dish. Layer the provolone cheese slices over the top of the rolls in the pan, followed by a generous layer of the roast beef. Place the top half of the cut rolls on top of the roast beef.

4. In a small bowl, combine the remaining 2 tablespoons of melted butter, the garlic powder, and the dried onion flakes. Brush over the tops of the rolls.

5. Cover the baking dish with foil, and bake for 25 minutes or until the cheese is melted and the meat is warmed.

6. Remove the foil, and cook for 5 more minutes so the tops of the rolls are slightly toasted.

7. Prepare the au jus sauce mix according to the package directions.

8. Cut the rolls into individual sliders, and serve warm with the au jus sauce on the side.

NOTE

You can use any type of cheese you prefer. If you want to make your sliders extra cheesy, you can add a second layer of cheese on top of the meat.

To view on device

CAJUN SHRIMP AND SAUSAGE VEGETABLE SHEET PAN

| SERVES 4 |

Experience a flavor-packed meal with this easy sheet-pan recipe. Simply toss shrimp, sliced sausage, and colorful veggies in a blend of olive oil and Cajun seasoning and then roast them to perfection in the oven.

PREP TIME	COOK TIME	TOTAL TIME
5 minutes	*20 minutes*	*25 minutes*

1. Preheat the oven to 400°F (205°C).

2. In a large bowl, add the shrimp, sausage, zucchini, yellow squash, asparagus, and red bell pepper.

3. Add the olive oil and Cajun seasoning, and toss to coat evenly.

4. Spread the shrimp, sausage, and veggies evenly onto a baking sheet. Bake for 15 to 20 minutes or until the shrimp is pink and the vegetables are tender.

5. Season with salt and black pepper, if needed, and serve.

1 lb (450g) large shrimp, peeled and deveined

14oz (400g) pork or chicken sausage, sliced

1 medium zucchini, sliced

1 medium yellow squash, sliced

½ bunch asparagus stalks, sliced into thirds

1 red bell pepper, ribs and seeds removed, and chopped

2 tbsp olive oil

2 tbsp Cajun seasoning

Salt and freshly ground black pepper

To view on device

TACO-STUFFED AVOCADOS

| SERVES 6 |

You'll love this healthy twist on classic tacos. Fresh avocados are packed with seasoned taco meat and topped with veggies, making every single bite creamy and delicious!

PREP TIME	COOK TIME	TOTAL TIME
5 minutes	*11 minutes*	*16 minutes*

1. In a medium saucepan over medium heat, cook and crumble the ground beef for 5 to 7 minutes or until browned. Drain the grease.

2. Add the chili powder, salt, cumin, oregano, garlic powder, onion powder, and tomato sauce to the beef. Stir to combine, and cook for about 3 or 4 minutes.

3. Into the hole where the avocado pit was, spoon some taco meat. Top with cheddar cheese, Roma tomatoes, red onions, black olives, and cilantro, and serve.

NOTE

If you want to make a larger hole in the avocado to fit more toppings, you can spoon out some of the avocado and use it to make fresh guacamole.

1 lb (450g) ground beef

1 tbsp chili powder

½ tsp salt

¾ tsp ground cumin

½ tsp dried oregano

¼ tsp garlic powder

¼ tsp onion powder

4oz (115g) tomato sauce

3 avocados, halved and pitted

1 cup shredded cheddar cheese

¼ cup chopped Roma tomatoes

¼ cup chopped red onion

½ cup sliced black olives

Chopped fresh cilantro, for garnish

To view on device

CUBAN SANDWICHES

| SERVES 8 |

With a mouthwatering combination of flavors, Cuban sandwiches
make the best lunch. The pork tenderloin, topped with the works, is nestled
between slices of delicious Cuban bread and then toasted in butter for a crispy
outside and perfectly melted cheese. This sandwich will be your new favorite!

PREP TIME	COOK TIME	TOTAL TIME
20 minutes	*40 minutes*	*1 hour*

1 lb (450g) pork tenderloin

¼ cup olive oil

¼ cup orange juice

2 tbsp lime juice

3 cloves garlic, minced

1 tsp dried oregano

½ tsp ground cumin

2 loaves Cuban bread
   (Italian bread also works.)

1 lb (450g) sliced Swiss cheese

1 lb (450g) sliced smoked ham

1 cup sliced dill pickles

¼ cup mustard

2 tbsp unsalted butter

1. Preheat the oven to 375°F (190°C). Line a rimmed baking sheet with foil.

2. Place the pork tenderloin on the prepared baking sheet.

3. In a small bowl, whisk together the olive oil, orange juice, lime juice, garlic, oregano, and cumin. Pour the marinade over the pork, and turn over the pork to coat both sides.

4. Cook for 25 to 30 minutes or until the meat reaches an internal temperature of 145°F (63°C). Thinly slice the meat, and set aside.

5. Slice each loaf of Cuban bread in half lengthwise. On the bottom halves of the bread, begin layering the ingredients: add half of the Swiss cheese, and top with the smoked ham, sliced pork, and dill pickles. Place the remaining Swiss cheese on top. Spread the mustard on the top pieces of bread, and place them on the sandwiches. Cut each loaf into four equal parts (8 sandwiches total).

6. In a large skillet or on a griddle over medium heat, melt the butter. Add the sandwiches, working in batches as necessary, and set a heavy skillet (such as cast-iron) on top of the sandwiches to press them down. Cook for 2 or 3 minutes. Flip over the sandwiches, and cook for 2 or 3 more minutes. Serve hot.

NOTE

If you have a panini press, you can use it to toast and press the sandwiches instead of using the skillet or griddle.

To view on device

AIR-FRYER TURKEY BURGERS

| SERVES 4 |

These juicy, flavorful turkey burgers are a healthier alternative to traditional beef burgers. Plus, they're cooked in an air fryer, making them an ideal option for a delicious, guilt-free burger.

PREP TIME	COOK TIME	TOTAL TIME
5 minutes	*25 minutes*	*20 minutes*

1. In a medium bowl, combine the turkey, garlic, salt, black pepper, and Worcestershire sauce. Shape the mixture into 4 patties, keeping them ½ inch (1.25cm) thick because they will shrink when cooked.

2. Add two patties to the air-fryer basket at a time, and cook at 360°F (180°C) for 7 minutes. Flip over the patties, and cook for 5 more minutes or until cooked through.

3. Add your desired toppings, and serve on whole-wheat buns.

1 lb (450g) ground turkey

3 cloves garlic, minced

Salt and freshly ground black pepper

1 tbsp Worcestershire sauce

4 whole-wheat hamburger buns

OPTIONAL TOPPINGS

Butter lettuce leaves

Heirloom tomato slices

Sprouts

Red onion slices

To view on device

QUICK AND EASY STROMBOLI

| SERVES 6 |

This mouthwatering classic is filled with Italian salami, pepperoni, and melted mozzarella cheese. This easy-to-make version is wrapped in pizza dough and baked until golden brown, creating a flavorful delight you'll want to make again and again.

PREP TIME	COOK TIME	TOTAL TIME
10 minutes	*20 minutes*	*30 minutes*

1 (13.8oz/391g) tube refrigerated pizza dough

½ cup pizza sauce

12 slices Italian salami

1¼ cups shredded mozzarella cheese

16 slices pepperoni

1 egg, beaten

1 tsp **Easy Italian Seasoning** (page 263)

2 tbsp grated Parmesan cheese

2 tbsp chopped fresh parsley (optional)

1. Preheat the oven to 400°F (205°C). Line a baking sheet with parchment paper.

2. Roll out the pizza dough, and stretch it to fill the prepared baking sheet. Spread the pizza sauce on the dough, leaving about 2 inches (5cm) from the edge sauce-free.

3. Top the sauce with Italian salami slices, followed by the mozzarella cheese, and then the pepperoni slices.

4. Roll up the dough like a cinnamon roll, and pinch the edges to seal and fold where the seam is. Lay the stromboli seam side down on the baking sheet.

5. Brush with the beaten egg, and cut small slits across the top with a sharp knife. Sprinkle the Easy Italian Seasoning and Parmesan cheese over the top of the stromboli.

6. Bake for 15 to 20 minutes or until golden brown on top. Garnish with parsley, if using, slice, and serve with more warm pizza sauce for dipping.

To view on device

FRESH CUCUMBER SANDWICHES

| SERVES 4 |

This is a delightful twist on the classic cucumber sandwich, with a creamy
and zesty spread made from cream cheese, mayonnaise, and herbs that perfectly
complement the cool, crisp slices of cucumber. It's the perfect sandwich for lunch.

PREP TIME
5 minutes

COOK TIME
None

TOTAL TIME
5 minutes

8oz (225g) cream cheese, softened

2 tbsp mayonnaise

1 tbsp lemon juice

1 tbsp chopped fresh chives or
green onions

1 tbsp chopped fresh dill

1 tsp chopped fresh parsley

Salt and freshly ground black pepper

8 slices white bread, crusts removed

2 medium or large cucumbers,
peeled and sliced

1. In a medium bowl, combine the cream cheese, mayonnaise, lemon juice, chives, dill, parsley, salt, and black pepper.

2. Spread the mixture on one side of four slices of bread.

3. Layer the cucumber slices on top of the cream cheese mixture and then top with the remaining slices of bread.

4. Cut each sandwich in half diagonally, and serve immediately.

To view on device

OVEN-BAKED
SHEET-PAN NACHOS

| SERVES 6 |

This family-friendly recipe features seasoned ground beef, refried beans, corn, black olives, black beans, salsa, and a blend of mild cheddar and Colby Jack cheeses, resulting in a cheesy, taco-nacho bake that's perfect for the whole family.

PREP TIME	COOK TIME	TOTAL TIME
5 minutes	*22 minutes*	*27 minutes*

1. Preheat the oven to 400°F (205°C).

2. In a medium skillet over medium heat, cook and crumble the ground beef for about 5 to 7 minutes or until browned. Drain the grease from the skillet, remove from the heat, and stir in The Best Homemade Taco Seasoning.

3. Arrange the tortilla chips in an even layer on a 15×10×1-inch (38×25.5×2.5cm) baking sheet. Spoon the refried beans evenly over the chips, followed by the taco meat. Sprinkle the corn, black olives, black beans, salsa, cheddar cheese, and Colby Jack cheese over the top. If you're using fresh jalapeños, add them now so they can roast. (Canned or jarred jalapeños can be added after baking.)

4. Bake for about 12 to 15 minutes or until the cheeses are fully melted.

5. Top with cilantro, sour cream, and Roma tomatoes, or your desired toppings, and serve warm.

1 lb (450g) ground beef

2 ½ tbsp **The Best Homemade Taco Seasoning** (page 265) or 1 (1oz/30g) packet

1 (13oz/370g) bag tortilla chips

1 (15oz/425g) can refried beans

½ cup cooked corn

½ cup sliced black olives

½ cup black beans

½ cup salsa

1 cup shredded mild cheddar cheese

1 cup shredded Colby Jack cheese

1 fresh jalapeño, deseeded and diced

Chopped fresh cilantro

Sour cream

Chopped Roma tomatoes

To view on device

BLACKENED CHICKEN AVOCADO POWER BOWLS

| SERVES 4 |

I love when I can take a break for lunch during the day and have a healthy meal filled with veggies. This power bowl has all my favorite healthy ingredients, like avocado, chickpeas, cabbage, and other roasted veggies. They are seasoned to perfection and have so much flavor that you will eat every last morsel.

PREP TIME	COOK TIME	TOTAL TIME
15 minutes	*20 minutes*	*35 minutes*

1. Preheat the oven to 425°F (220°C).

2. In a small bowl, combine the chili powder, sweet paprika, onion powder, cumin, garlic powder, Easy Italian Seasoning, salt, and black pepper.

3. Coat the chicken breasts with about 1 tablespoon of the olive oil, and rub the spice mixture evenly on the front and back of each breast.

4. In a medium skillet over medium-high heat, heat 1 tablespoon olive oil. Add the chicken, and cook for 2 or 3 minutes per side or until cooked.

5. Arrange the broccoli, red and yellow bell peppers, and chickpeas in a single layer on a baking sheet. Drizzle with remaining 2 tablespoons olive oil and then sprinkle with salt and pepper. Roast for 15 minutes or until tender.

6. Slice the cooked chicken into strips. Evenly divide it and the broccoli, bell peppers, chickpeas, avocado, and red cabbage among 4 bowls, and serve.

1 tbsp chili powder

2 tsp sweet paprika

1 tsp onion powder

1 tsp ground cumin

½ tsp garlic powder

1 tsp **Easy Italian Seasoning** (page 263)

1 tsp salt

¼ tsp freshly ground black pepper

4 boneless, skinless chicken breasts (about 1½ lb/680g), thinly sliced

4 tbsp olive oil

2 cups broccoli florets

1 red bell pepper, ribs and seeds removed, and sliced

1 yellow bell pepper, ribs and seeds removed, and sliced

1 (15oz/425g) can chickpeas (garbanzo beans), drained and rinsed

1 avocado, pitted and diced

1 cup chopped red cabbage

To view on device

ULTIMATE TUNA MELT

| SERVES 8 |

If you are looking for a delicious sandwich that fills you up and tastes like it came from a restaurant, this is it! This melt features a flavorful tuna filling, gooey cheddar cheese, and freshly sliced tomatoes all melted together between thick slices of crispy, golden bread.

PREP TIME
10 minutes

COOK TIME
5 minutes

TOTAL TIME
15 minutes

3 (5oz/142g) cans tuna, drained

¼ cup mayonnaise

¼ cup finely chopped celery

¼ cup finely chopped red onion

1 tbsp Dijon mustard

2 tbsp chopped fresh parsley

Salt and freshly ground black pepper

¼ cup unsalted butter, softened

16 thick slices bread

8 slices cheddar cheese

2 heirloom tomatoes, sliced

1. In a medium bowl, combine the tuna, mayonnaise, celery, red onion, Dijon mustard, and parsley. Season to taste with salt and black pepper.

2. Butter one side of each slice of bread. Place each slice of bread butter side down, and add 1 slice of cheddar cheese on the unbuttered side. Add a scoop of the tuna mixture on top of the cheese, top the tuna mixture with 1 tomato slice, and place a second slice of bread, butter side up, on the tomato. (You can place a second slice of cheese on top of the tomato if you like; in this case, you'll need 16 cheese slices.)

3. Preheat a medium skillet over medium heat. Add the sandwich, and cook for 2 or 3 minutes or until the cheese is melted and the bread is golden brown. Flip the sandwich, and cook for 2 or 3 more minutes or until the bread is golden brown.

NOTE

You can cook the sandwiches under the broiler instead of on the stovetop if you prefer. Simply preheat the broiler, place the sandwich on a baking sheet, and broil for 2 or 3 minutes or until the cheese is melted. Serve immediately.

To view on device

ASIAN TURKEY LETTUCE WRAPS

| SERVES 8 |

You'll love the flavors of this Asian-inspired dish. Ground turkey is mixed with fresh veggies and finished with a delicious blend of hoisin sauce, soy sauce, rice wine vinegar, and red chili paste. The savory mixture is served on crisp butter lettuce leaves for a refreshing meal.

PREP TIME	COOK TIME	TOTAL TIME
10 minutes	*11 minutes*	*21 minutes*

1 tbsp sesame oil

1 lb (450g) ground turkey

¼ cup shredded carrots

6oz (170g) shiitake mushrooms, coarsely chopped

1 (8oz/225g) can sliced water chestnuts, drained and coarsely chopped

2 green onions, chopped

1 clove garlic, minced

¼ cup hoisin sauce

2 tbsp low-sodium soy sauce

1 tbsp rice wine vinegar

2 tsp red chili paste

12 butter lettuce leaves (Boston or iceberg lettuce leaves also work.)

Chopped fresh parsley, for garnish

Crushed red pepper flakes, for garnish (optional)

1. In a medium skillet over medium-high heat, add the sesame oil and turkey. Cook, crumbling, for 5 to 7 minutes or until the turkey is almost cooked.

2. Add the carrots, shiitake mushrooms, water chestnuts, green onions, and garlic, and cook for 1 or 2 minutes until the turkey is cooked and the veggies are tender.

3. In a small bowl, combine the hoisin sauce, soy sauce, rice wine vinegar, and chili paste. Stir into the turkey and vegetable mix, and simmer for 1 or 2 minutes.

4. Serve warm on butter lettuce leaves, garnished with parsley and crushed red pepper flakes, if using.

To view on device

CHICKEN PARMESAN SANDWICHES

| SERVES 4 |

Packed with flavor, this sandwich is made with deliciously breaded chicken that's fried to perfection and then topped with melted cheese, fresh basil, and fresh marinara sauce. You'll enjoy every bite.

2 boneless, skinless chicken breasts, sliced in half lengthwise

¾ tsp plus ½ tsp salt

¾ tsp **Easy Italian Seasoning** (page 263)

¼ cup all-purpose flour

2 eggs

½ tsp garlic powder

1 cup panko breadcrumbs

½ cup grated Parmesan cheese

1½ cups vegetable or canola oil, for frying

4 hoagie rolls

2 tbsp unsalted butter, softened

8 slices fresh mozzarella cheese

1 cup warm **Homemade Marinara Sauce** (page 263)

Fresh basil leaves

PREP TIME	COOK TIME	TOTAL TIME
15 minutes	*15 minutes*	*25 minutes*

1. Preheat the broiler to high.

2. Sprinkle the chicken with ¾ teaspoon salt and Easy Italian Seasoning.

3. Create a breading station by placing the all-purpose flour on a plate. In a deep dish, whisk together the eggs, the remaining ½ teaspoon salt, and the garlic powder. Mix the panko breadcrumbs and Parmesan cheese on another plate.

4. Dust a piece of chicken with the flour. Dip it into the egg mixture, and shake off the excess egg. Coat the chicken in the Parmesan-panko mixture. Place the breaded chicken on a wire rack, and repeat with the remaining chicken.

5. In a large skillet over medium-high heat, heat the vegetable oil to 350°F (175°C). Place 2 chicken breasts gently in the oil, and fry for 2½ minutes per side or until golden brown. Transfer to the wire rack, and repeat with the remaining chicken.

6. Cut the hoagie rolls in half lengthwise. Spread each cut side of the bread with butter, and place them on a baking sheet. Broil for about 1 or 2 minutes or until toasted.

7. Spread warm Homemade Marinara Sauce on both sides of the chicken. Place 1 piece of chicken on the bottom half of each hoagie, top with 2 slices fresh mozzarella cheese, and return to the broiler for 1 or 2 more minutes or until the cheese has melted. Add fresh basil on top of the melted cheese, add the top of the hoagies, and serve.

CRISPY PARMESAN AIR-FRYER CHICKEN TENDERS

| SERVES 4 |

These chicken tenders are crispy and golden outside and tender and juicy inside, with a hint of garlic and tons of flavor. They're a perfect choice for a simple yet satisfying meal, especially when paired with my **Famous Fry Sauce** (page 264).

PREP TIME	COOK TIME	TOTAL TIME
5 minutes	*20 minutes*	*25 minutes*

1. Trim the fat from the chicken tenders.

2. In one shallow bowl, combine the all-purpose flour, salt, and black pepper. In a second shallow bowl, mix together the olive oil and garlic. In a third shallow bowl, combine the basil, sweet paprika, panko breadcrumbs, and Parmesan cheese.

3. Evenly and thoroughly coat each tender in the flour mixture, dredge in the garlic oil, and coat in the panko mixture.

4. Place the tenders in the air-fryer basket, and cook at 400°F (205°C) for 9 minutes. Flip over the tenders, and cook for 8 or 9 more minutes or until the internal temperature of the chicken reaches 165°F (75°C).

5. Serve immediately with the Famous Fry Sauce, if using, or your favorite dipping sauce.

1¼ lb (565g) boneless, skinless chicken tenders

½ cup all-purpose flour

½ tsp salt

¼ tsp freshly ground black pepper

6 tbsp olive oil or melted unsalted butter

3 tsp minced garlic

1 tsp dried basil

¼ tsp sweet paprika

1 cup panko breadcrumbs

⅔ cup freshly grated Parmesan cheese

Famous Fry Sauce (page 264, optional)

To view on device

SOUPS & SALADS

From warm, filling soups to healthy and refreshing salads, these recipes are favorites in our household all year round. When we're at the cabin during the cold winter months, we love to prepare comforting classics like **Broccoli Cheese Soup** (page 104) and the timeless favorite, **The Best Chicken Noodle Soup** (page 91). And no gathering is complete without the delightful **Fluffy Strawberry Cheesecake Salad** (page 102) or the irresistible **Incredible Bacon Ranch Pasta Salad** (page 95) for pasta lovers. Don't miss out on the vibrant and zesty **Greek Salad with Lemon Yogurt Dressing** (page 98). Each recipe brings together a perfect balance of flavors and textures.

◀ *Winter is such a magical time for me at our cabin. After you have been sledding and snowmobiling all day, I can guarantee you that I will be back at the cabin making you a warm bowl of soup. Broccoli Cheese Soup is one of our favorite soups and is so warm and comforting after playing in the snow. Nothing beats a good soup and salad at the cabin.*

SLOW COOKER PASTA E FAGIOLI SOUP

| SERVES 10 |

This rich and hearty Italian soup is loaded with pasta, vegetables, beans, and lean ground beef. It's made in a slow cooker, so it's easy to make and oh so delicious.

PREP TIME	COOK TIME	TOTAL TIME
10 minutes	*8 hours*	*8 hours 10 minutes*

1. In a large skillet over medium heat, cook the ground beef in the olive oil for 7 to 10 minutes or until browned and no longer pink.

2. Transfer the beef to a 5-quart (4.75-liter) slow cooker. Add the carrots, celery, white onion, crushed tomatoes, beef broth, Easy Italian Seasoning, bay leaves, salt, and black pepper.

3. Cover and cook on low for 7 or 8 hours or on high for 3 or 4 hours.

4. About 30 minutes before serving, stir in the cannellini beans, kidney beans, and ditalini pasta.

5. Remove and discard the bay leaves. Season with salt and pepper, and serve hot.

1 lb (450g) lean ground beef

1 tbsp olive oil

2 carrots, diced

4 celery stalks, diced

1 medium white onion, diced

1 (28oz/800g) can crushed tomatoes

2 (14.5oz/410g) cans beef broth

1 tbsp **Easy Italian Seasoning** (page 263)

2 bay leaves

1 tsp salt, plus more to taste

¼ tsp freshly ground black pepper, plus more to taste

1 (15oz/425g) can cannellini beans, drained and rinsed

1 (15oz/425g) can dark or light red kidney beans, drained and rinsed

1 cup uncooked ditalini pasta

To view on device

HONEY LIME POPPY SEED FRUIT SALAD

| SERVES 10 |

This refreshing fruit salad features a colorful medley of fruit dressed
with a sweet and tangy glaze made from honey, lime juice, and poppy seeds.
Garnished with chopped fresh mint, it's a delightful summer treat bursting with flavor.

PREP TIME	COOK TIME	TOTAL TIME
10 minutes	*None*	*10 minutes*

1 cup sliced strawberries

½ cup blackberries

½ cup blueberries

½ cup peeled and sliced kiwi

½ cup cubed mango

1 tbsp honey

3 tbsp lime juice

1 tbsp poppy seeds

Chopped fresh mint, for garnish

1. In a large bowl, add the strawberries, blackberries, blueberries, kiwi, and mango.

2. In a small bowl, whisk together the honey, lime juice, and poppy seeds.

3. Drizzle the honey lime poppy seed glaze over the fruit, and gently toss to coat. Garnish with mint and serve immediately.

To view on device

STRAWBERRY AVOCADO SPINACH SALAD
with Creamy Poppy Seed Dressing

| SERVES 8 |

This is my all-time favorite salad. I love the sweet and tangy poppy seed dressing combined with the fresh strawberries, creamy avocado, and crunch from the almonds. This salad can be eaten all year round, and at our house, it is!

PREP TIME
10 minutes

COOK TIME
None

TOTAL TIME
10 minutes

FOR THE SALAD

5 cups baby spinach

1 cup freshly sliced strawberries

2 large avocados, pitted and chopped

¼ cup sliced almonds, plus more for garnish (optional)

¼ cup crumbled feta cheese, plus more for garnish (optional)

FOR THE DRESSING

⅓ cup mayonnaise

¼ cup 2% milk

3 tbsp granulated sugar

4 tsp apple cider vinegar

2 tsp poppy seeds

1. In a large salad bowl, combine the baby spinach, strawberries, avocados, almonds, and feta cheese.

2. In a small bowl, whisk together the mayonnaise, milk, sugar, apple cider vinegar, and poppy seeds. Pour about half of the dressing over the salad, and toss to coat. Add more dressing if needed, and store any leftover dressing in an airtight container in the refrigerator for up to 7 days.

3. Garnish with additional feta cheese and almonds, if using, and serve immediately.

To view on device

CREAMY ZUPPA TOSCANA

| SERVES 10 |

This is a hearty and creamy soup made with bacon, sausage, kale, and all sorts of delicious seasonings. It's the perfect combination of flavors that will warm you up on a chilly day.

PREP TIME
10 minutes

COOK TIME
23 minutes

TOTAL TIME
33 minutes

1 lb (450g) Italian sausage

4 medium russet potatoes

3 (14oz/400g) cans chicken broth

1 medium white onion, diced

2 cloves garlic, minced

½ lb (225g) bacon, crisp-cooked, drained, and crumbled

2½ cups chopped kale or spinach

2 cups heavy cream

Salt and freshly ground black pepper

1. In a medium skillet over medium-high heat, cook the Italian sausage for 8 to 10 minutes or until browned. Remove from the heat, and set aside.

2. Peel the russet potatoes, slice them in half, and cut into about ¼-inch (0.5cm) chunks. (Or cut them into fourths to make the potatoes more bite size.)

3. Add the chicken broth to a large pot, set over medium-high heat, and bring to a boil. Add the potatoes, and boil for about 10 minutes or until tender.

4. Meanwhile, in a small skillet over medium heat, sauté the white onion and garlic for about 5 to 7 minutes or until tender. Remove from the heat.

5. When the potatoes are tender, add the sausage, onion, bacon, and kale to the pot. Boil for 2 or 3 minutes or until the kale starts to wilt.

6. Reduce the heat to low, add the heavy cream, and cook for 10 minutes or until heated through. Season with salt and black pepper, and serve.

To view on device

AVOCADO BASIL PASTA SALAD

| SERVES 4 |

Bursting with flavor, this delightful pasta salad pairs creamy avocados
and fresh basil with pasta, tomatoes, bacon, lemon, and garlic. Top it
off with shredded Parmesan cheese for an irresistible dish.

PREP TIME
10 minutes + 30 minutes to cool

COOK TIME
10 minutes

TOTAL TIME
50 minutes

8oz (225g) uncooked bow tie or
wagon wheel pasta

2 medium avocados, peeled, pitted,
and coarsely chopped

2 medium Roma tomatoes, roughly
chopped

6 slices bacon, crisp-cooked, drained,
and crumbled

2/3 cup freshly chopped basil

2 tbsp lemon juice

1 tbsp olive oil

3 cloves garlic, minced

1/8 tsp salt

1/4 tsp freshly ground black pepper

1/2 cup shredded Parmesan cheese

1. In a large pot, cook the pasta in boiling water according to the package directions. Drain, rinse with cool water, and set aside.

2. In a large bowl, combine the avocados, Roma tomatoes, bacon, basil, lemon juice, olive oil, garlic, salt, and black pepper. Add the cooked pasta, and toss to combine.

3. Transfer to a serving bowl, sprinkle with Parmesan cheese, and set in the refrigerator to cool for about 30 minutes before serving. Store any leftovers in an airtight container in the refrigerator for up to 4 days.

To view on device

STRAWBERRY PRETZEL SALAD

| SERVES 16 |

This delicious salad doubles as a dessert, with its buttery pretzel crust, layer of sweet cream, and vibrant layer of strawberry gelatin dessert generously studded with slices of juicy strawberries.

PREP TIME
10 minutes
+ 5 hours 30 minutes
to cool and set

COOK TIME
10 minutes

TOTAL TIME
5 hours 50 minutes

2 ½ cups crushed pretzels

3 tbsp packed brown sugar

¾ cup melted unsalted butter

1 (6oz/170g) package instant strawberry gelatin dessert

8oz (225g) softened cream cheese

1 cup granulated sugar

8oz (225g) frozen whipped topping, thawed

1 lb (450g) fresh strawberries, sliced

1. Preheat the oven to 350°F (175°C). Lightly coat a 9×13-inch (23×33cm) baking pan with cooking spray.

2. In a large bowl, combine the crushed pretzels, brown sugar, and butter. Evenly press the crust mixture into the bottom of the prepared baking pan, and bake for 8 minutes. Remove from the oven, and let cool completely.

3. Meanwhile, make the strawberry gelatin dessert according to the package directions. Let it sit at room temperature for 1 hour or until it cools.

4. In a medium bowl, and using a mixer on medium, beat together the cream cheese and granulated sugar until creamy.

5. Using a rubber spatula, fold in the whipped topping. Spread the mixture evenly over the pretzel crust, completely to the edges so the gelatin dessert won't leak through when it's added later. Set in the refrigerator to cool for 30 minutes.

6. After the gelatin dessert has cooled to room temperature, layer the sliced strawberries over the chilled cream layer and pour the gelatin dessert over the top. Refrigerate for 4 hours or overnight before serving. Store any leftovers in an airtight container in the refrigerator for up to 4 days.

NOTE

This is an easy recipe to customize. Try an orange pretzel salad—with orange gelatin dessert, 8 ounces (225g) crushed pineapple, and 8 ounces (225g) mandarin oranges—or any fruit and gelatin dessert flavor combinations you like.

To view on device

THE BEST CHICKEN NOODLE SOUP

| SERVES 8 |

This comforting chicken noodle soup combines tender carrots, celery, and
onion with aromatic garlic and fresh thyme and is simmered in a flavorful broth.
Wide egg noodles and shredded chicken complete this hearty and satisfying soup.

PREP TIME
15 minutes

COOK TIME
20 minutes

TOTAL TIME
35 minutes

4 large carrots, sliced

4 celery stalks, sliced

1 small white onion, diced

2 tbsp olive oil

3 cloves garlic, minced

2 tbsp fresh thyme, stems removed

Salt and freshly ground black pepper

10 cups chicken broth

12oz (340g) uncooked wide egg noodles

2 cups cooked and shredded chicken

2 tbsp chopped fresh parsley

1. In a large pot over medium-high heat, sauté the carrots, celery, and onion in the olive oil for 4 or 5 minutes or until the vegetables are tender.

2. Add the garlic, thyme, salt, and black pepper, and sauté for 1 minute.

3. Add the chicken broth and egg noodles, increase the heat to high, and boil for 8 to 10 minutes or until the noodles are al dente.

4. Add the chicken and parsley right before serving, and simmer for 4 or 5 minutes or until the chicken is heated. Season with additional salt and pepper, and serve hot.

To view on device

CHEESEBURGER SOUP

| SERVES 6 |

This thick and hearty soup is full of lean, tender ground beef and creamy cheese;
potatoes, carrots, and celery add a serving of vegetables, too. It's easy to make,
and it feeds a crowd—it's my go-to soup during cold winter months!

PREP TIME
15 minutes

COOK TIME
30 minutes

TOTAL TIME
45 minutes

1 lb (450g) lean ground beef

4 tbsp unsalted butter

½ cup chopped white onion

1 cup shredded carrots

½ cup diced celery

1 tbsp **Easy Italian Seasoning**
(page 263)

3 cups chicken broth

4 cups peeled and diced russet
potatoes

¼ cup all-purpose flour

2 cups Velveeta cheese, cubed, or
2 cups shredded cheddar cheese

1½ cups 2% milk

¾ tsp salt

¼ tsp freshly ground black pepper

¼ cup sour cream

1 tbsp Dijon mustard

1. In a large saucepan over medium heat, cook the ground beef for
5 minutes or until browned. Drain, transfer beef to a bowl, and set aside.

2. In the same saucepan, add 1 tablespoon butter, white onion, carrots,
celery, and Easy Italian Seasoning. Sauté for 3 or 4 minutes or
until tender.

3. Add the chicken broth, russet potatoes, and browned beef, and bring to
a boil. Reduce the heat to low, cover, and simmer for 10 to 12 minutes
or until potatoes are tender.

4. In a small skillet over medium heat, melt the remaining 3 tablespoons
butter. Add the all-purpose flour, and cook, stirring, for 3 to 5 minutes
or until bubbly.

5. Add the flour mixture to the soup, increase the heat to medium-high, and
bring to a boil. Cook, stirring, for 2 minutes. Reduce the heat to low.

6. Stir in the Velveeta, milk, salt, and black pepper. Cook, stirring, for
2 more minutes or until the cheese melts.

7. Remove from the heat, blend in the sour cream and Dijon mustard, and
serve warm.

To view on device

INCREDIBLE BACON RANCH PASTA SALAD

| SERVES 12 |

If you are looking for a delicious pasta salad you can serve all year long and for any occasion, this is it! Packed with salty bacon and colorful veggies that have perfectly contrasting textures and flavors, every bite is satisfying.

PREP TIME
15 minutes

COOK TIME
10 minutes

TOTAL TIME
25 minutes

16oz (450g) uncooked tricolor fusilli pasta, or your choice

10 slices bacon, crisp-cooked, drained, and crumbled

3 Roma tomatoes, diced

2 cups chopped fresh broccoli florets

5oz (140g) sliced black olives

2 cups shredded cheddar cheese

1 cup mayonnaise

1 (1.5oz/43g) packet dry ranch seasoning

1. In a large pot, cook the fusilli pasta in boiling water according to the package directions. Drain and rinse in cold water.

2. In a large bowl, combine the pasta, cooked bacon, Roma tomatoes, broccoli, black olives, and cheddar cheese.

3. In a small bowl, whisk together the mayonnaise and ranch seasoning.

4. Add the dressing to the pasta and veggies, stir to combine, and serve immediately. Store any leftovers in an airtight container in the refrigerator for up to 4 days.

NOTE

For a slightly healthier version, you can substitute 1 cup Greek yogurt for the mayonnaise.

To view on device

8-CAN CHICKEN TACO SOUP

| SERVES 8 |

You are going to fall in love with this quick and easy soup recipe.
It's packed full of flavor, the ingredients come right from your pantry, and it's
the perfect dinner when there's no time to run to the grocery store but the family needs
dinner *now*. I love topping it off with some extra veggies and tortilla strips for crunch.

PREP TIME	COOK TIME	TOTAL TIME
5 minutes	*10 minutes*	*15 minutes*

1 (15oz/425g) can diced tomatoes

1 (15oz/425g) can corn, drained

1 (15oz/425g) can black beans, drained and rinsed

1 (15oz/425g) can pinto beans, drained and rinsed

1 (10.5oz/300g) can cream of chicken soup

1 (12oz/340g) can chicken breast, drained

To view on device

1 (10oz/285g) can green enchilada sauce

1 (15oz/425g) can chicken broth

2 tbsp **The Best Homemade Taco Seasoning** (page 265), or 1 (1oz/30g) packet

OPTIONAL TOPPINGS

Sliced black olives

Avocado slices

Tortilla strips

Sour cream

Lime wedges

Fresh cilantro

1. In a large pan over medium-high heat, combine the diced tomatoes, corn, black beans, pinto beans, cream of chicken soup, chicken breast, green enchilada sauce, chicken broth, and The Best Homemade Taco Seasoning.

2. Bring to a boil, reduce the heat to medium, and simmer for 5 to 10 minutes.

3. Serve with your desired toppings.

WILD RICE AND MUSHROOM SOUP

COOKBOOK EXCLUSIVE

| SERVES 6 |

This soup has a blend of deeply caramelized onions combined with wild rice, button mushrooms, and a delicious variety of spices. It's the perfect starter for any meal or can be served as an entrée in cold winter months.

PREP TIME	COOK TIME	TOTAL TIME
10 minutes	*50 minutes*	*60 minutes*

2 tbsp olive oil

1 lb (450g) button mushrooms, sliced

3 cloves garlic, minced

¼ cup unsalted butter

1 small white onion, diced

2 carrots, peeled and chopped

2 celery stalks, diced

1 tbsp chopped fresh thyme

1 tsp dried sage

1 tsp kosher salt, plus more to taste

¼ tsp freshly ground black pepper

2 tbsp all-purpose flour

1 cup uncooked wild rice blend

8 cups chicken stock

1. In a large Dutch oven over medium-high heat, heat the olive oil. Add the button mushrooms, and sauté for 4 or 5 minutes or until they release their liquids. Continue to sauté for 8 to 10 more minutes or until they caramelize and the liquid cooks off and turns golden brown.

2. Add the garlic, and cook, stirring, for 1 minute.

3. Add the butter, white onion, carrots, and celery. Sauté for 3 or 4 minutes or until the vegetables start to soften. Reduce the heat to medium.

4. Add the thyme, sage, kosher salt, and black pepper, and stir. Add the all-purpose flour, and cook, stirring, for about 2 more minutes.

5. Add the wild rice blend and chicken stock. Increase the heat to high, and bring to a boil. Reduce the heat to low, cover, and let the rice simmer for 30 minutes or until tender.

GREEK SALAD
with Lemon Yogurt Dressing

| SERVES 6 |

Enjoy the flavors of the Mediterranean in this refreshing salad that combines
crisp romaine lettuce, fresh veggies, and tangy feta cheese with a creamy lemon dressing.
This salad is a perfect blend of textures and tastes and will go with any meal.

PREP TIME
15 minutes

COOK TIME
None

TOTAL TIME
15 minutes

3 cups chopped romaine lettuce

1 cucumber, seeded and sliced into ½ moons

1 green bell pepper, ribs and seeds removed, and chopped

2 Roma tomatoes, sliced

½ cup pitted Kalamata olives

½ cup large pitted black olives

8oz (225g) block feta cheese, cut into ½-in (1.25cm) cubes

FOR THE LEMON YOGURT DRESSING

½ cup plain Greek yogurt

½ cup extra-virgin olive oil

¼ cup lemon juice

1 clove garlic, minced

2 tbsp honey

½ tsp salt

¼ tsp freshly ground black pepper

1 tbsp minced fresh dill

1. In a large bowl, add the romaine lettuce, cucumber, green bell pepper, Roma tomatoes, Kalamata olives, black olives, and feta cheese.

2. To a small bowl, add the Greek yogurt, extra-virgin olive oil, lemon juice, garlic, honey, salt, black pepper, and dill, and whisk until smooth.

3. Drizzle the desired amount of dressing over the salad, toss to combine, and serve fresh.

MY GO-TO HOUSE SALAD

| SERVES 6 |

Everyone needs a salad they can make to go with any meal. This one is the absolute best.
It has homemade croutons, a delicious and zesty dressing, and a yummy mixture of veggies.
It makes the perfect starter or side dish, and I know it will become your go-to salad, too.

PREP TIME
15 minutes

COOK TIME
15 minutes

TOTAL TIME
30 minutes

FOR THE HOMEMADE CROUTONS

½ loaf crusty French bread, or bread of choice

¼ cup olive oil

2 tsp **Easy Italian Seasoning** (page 263)

⅛ tsp garlic salt

¼ cup grated Parmesan cheese

FOR THE SALAD

6 cups romaine lettuce, or mixed greens

2 Roma tomatoes, sliced and quartered

1 cup sliced and quartered cucumber

¼ cup sliced and halved red onion

1 cup homemade croutons

½ cup shredded Parmesan cheese

FOR THE ZESTY ITALIAN DRESSING

1 tbsp onion powder

1 tbsp granulated sugar

1 tbsp kosher salt

2 tbsp **Easy Italian Seasoning** (page 263)

1 tsp garlic powder

1 tsp freshly ground black pepper

¼ tsp celery salt

¾ cup extra-virgin olive oil

⅓ cup white vinegar

¼ cup water

2 tbsp mayonnaise

1. Preheat the oven to 400°F (205°C).

2. Slice the French bread into 1-inch (2.5cm) cubes. Add to a large bowl, drizzle with olive oil, and toss to coat.

3. Add the Easy Italian Seasoning, garlic salt, and Parmesan cheese, and toss to coat again.

4. Spread the croutons into an even layer on a baking sheet, and bake for 10 to 15 minutes or until toasted and golden brown.

5. In a large bowl, combine the romaine lettuce, Roma tomatoes, cucumber, red onion, croutons, and Parmesan cheese.

6. In a medium bowl, whisk together the dressing ingredients. Pour the dressing over the salad, top with the croutons, and serve.

FLUFFY STRAWBERRY CHEESECAKE SALAD

| SERVES 8 |

Perfect for warm days when you want something refreshing and sweet, this salad is easy
to make and will please any crowd. It's the biggest hit at every potluck I take it to.

PREP TIME
15 minutes + 1 hour chill time

COOK TIME
None

TOTAL TIME
1 hour 15 minutes

3 (6oz/170g) containers strawberry yogurt (2 cups)

1 (3.4oz/100g) package instant cheesecake pudding

8oz (225g) frozen whipped topping, thawed

1 lb (450g) fresh strawberries, sliced

2 cups miniature marshmallows

3 bananas, sliced

To view on device

1. In a large bowl, mix together the strawberry yogurt and cheesecake pudding powder. Fold in the whipped topping.

2. Cover and refrigerate for about 1 hour to set.

3. Just before serving, add the sliced strawberries, marshmallows, and bananas. Keep refrigerated, and store any leftovers in an airtight container in the refrigerator for up to 2 days.

NOTE

If you can't find instant cheesecake pudding, you can substitute 8 ounces (225g) softened cream cheese, ½ cup granulated sugar, and 2 cups heavy whipping cream for it and omit the frozen whipped topping. Beat the ingredients in a large bowl until creamy and stiff peaks form. Fold in the strawberry yogurt, strawberries, marshmallows, and bananas right before serving.

CALIFORNIA SPAGHETTI SALAD

| SERVES 12 |

This pasta salad is full of fresh veggies and coated in a zesty Italian dressing. With all those colors and flavors, it's as beautiful as it is delicious, and there's no doubt it will be the hit of your next gathering.

PREP TIME	COOK TIME	TOTAL TIME
5 minutes *+ 3 hours to chill*	*10 minutes*	*3 hours 15 minutes*

1. In a large pot, cook the thin spaghetti in boiling water according to the package directions. Drain using a colander, rinse in cold water, and add to a large bowl.

2. To the pasta, add the cherry tomatoes, cucumber, red bell pepper, red onion, and black olives.

3. To make the dressing, whisk together the Italian salad dressing, Parmesan cheese, sesame seeds, sweet paprika, celery seed, and garlic powder. Pour the dressing over the salad, and toss until coated. Cover and refrigerate for 3 hours or overnight before serving.

16oz (450g) uncooked thin spaghetti, broken into 1-in (2.5cm) pieces

1 pint (475g) cherry tomatoes, halved

1 cucumber, diced

1 red bell pepper, ribs and seeds removed, and diced

½ red onion, diced

1 (2.25oz/65g) can sliced black olives, drained

FOR THE DRESSING

1 (16oz/450g) bottle Italian salad dressing

¼ cup grated Parmesan cheese

1 tbsp sesame seeds

1 tsp sweet paprika

½ tsp celery seed

¼ tsp garlic powder

To view on device

BROCCOLI CHEESE SOUP

| SERVES 8 |

Our family loves spending time at our cabin in the wintertime, and after a long day of sledding and playing in the snow, this warm and flavorful soup hits the spot. It's quick and easy to make and so deliciously creamy. I love to serve it in a bread bowl so we can eat every last bite!

PREP TIME
15 minutes

COOK TIME
50 minutes

TOTAL TIME
1 hour 5 minutes

½ medium yellow onion, chopped

1 tbsp plus ¼ cup unsalted butter, melted

¼ cup all-purpose flour

2 cups half-and-half

2 cups chicken stock

½ lb (225g) fresh broccoli florets (about 1 cup)

1 cup julienned carrots

¼ tsp ground nutmeg

Salt and freshly ground black pepper

8oz (225g) grated sharp cheddar cheese

1. In a small pan, sauté the yellow onion in 1 tablespoon melted butter. Remove from the heat and set aside.

2. In a large pot over medium heat, whisk together the remaining ¼ cup melted butter and all-purpose flour. Cook, whisking, for about 3 or 4 minutes.

3. Slowly whisk in the half-and-half and chicken stock, and simmer for about 20 minutes.

4. Add the broccoli, carrots, and sautéed onions. Reduce the heat to medium-low, and simmer for about 25 minutes or until the broccoli and carrots are tender.

5. Add the nutmeg, salt, black pepper, and sharp cheddar cheese, and stir to combine. Let the cheese melt and then serve.

NOTE

For a smoother soup, you can use an immersion blender, or you can purée it in batches in a blender.

To view on device

STARTERS & APPETIZERS

This section is packed with a varied assortment of mouthwatering appetizer and starter recipes that are easy to make and sure to impress your guests. From the spicy **Jalapeño Bacon Cheeseball** (page 113) to the tangy **Thai Glazed Chicken Wings** (page 111), these dishes are full of flavor. Whether you're hosting a casual gathering or a special event, the crowd-pleasing **Hot Spinach Artichoke Dip** (page 129) and the delightful **Whipped Feta Dip** (page 132) are sure to be a hit.

◄ *Can we skip dinner and dessert and just have a spread of starters and dips? That is my heaven right there!*

CREAMY CHICKEN ALFREDO DIP

| SERVES 12 |

Chicken Alfredo is a classic flavor combination I couldn't wait to turn into an appetizer.
This hot dip checks all the boxes: it's creamy, cheesy, and loaded with bites of tasty
chicken. The flavor mimics one of my favorite Italian dishes, and once you dip
into it with a crostini (or any bread with a hard crust), you will love it, too.

PREP TIME
5 minutes

COOK TIME
20 minutes

TOTAL TIME
25 minutes

2 tbsp unsalted butter

2 tbsp all-purpose flour

3 cloves garlic, minced

1 cup 2% milk

8oz (225g) cream cheese

1½ cups shredded mozzarella cheese

¼ cup grated Parmesan cheese

1½ cups cooked and shredded chicken
(I use a rotisserie chicken.)

1 tsp **Easy Italian Seasoning**
(page 263)

½ tsp salt

¼ tsp freshly ground black pepper

1. Preheat the oven to 350°F (175°C).

2. In a small skillet over medium-high heat, melt the butter. Whisk in the all-purpose flour to create a roux (see **Note**).

3. Add the garlic and milk, and whisk until smooth. Reduce the heat to low, add the cream cheese, and stir until smooth and creamy.

4. Add 1 cup mozzarella cheese, the Parmesan cheese, chicken, Easy Italian Seasoning, salt, and black pepper, and stir until combined.

5. Top with the remaining ½ cup mozzarella, and bake for 20 to 25 minutes or until golden brown and bubbly. Serve with crostini, broccoli, or crackers.

NOTE

A *roux* is a mixture of flour and fat—in this case, butter—that is typically added to soups, sauces, and gravies to make them thick, smooth, and rich.

To view on device

SAUSAGE-STUFFED MUSHROOMS

| SERVES 10 |

These mushrooms, filled with a creamy mixture of onions, garlic, chopped mushroom stems, and sausage, are a great appetizer to feed a crowd. The best part is that they can be made in just 50 minutes. They're a must-make for your next party!

PREP TIME
10 minutes

COOK TIME
40 minutes

TOTAL TIME
50 minutes

24oz (680g) white button mushrooms

½ lb (225g) hot pork sausage

2 tbsp olive oil

¼ cup diced white onion

4 cloves garlic, minced

8oz (225g) cream cheese, softened

1 egg yolk

1 cup grated Parmesan cheese

2 tbsp finely chopped fresh parsley

Salt and freshly ground black pepper

To view on device

1. Preheat the oven to 350°F (175°C).

2. Pop off the white button mushroom stems, chop finely, and set aside.

3. In a medium skillet over medium-high heat, brown the hot pork sausage for 10 to 12 minutes. Drain, transfer to a plate, and set aside to cool.

4. In the same skillet, add the olive oil, white onion, garlic, and chopped mushroom stems. Sauté for about 3 minutes or until tender. Set aside to cool.

5. In a medium bowl, combine the cream cheese and egg yolk. Stir in the Parmesan cheese and parsley. Add the cooled sausage and the onion mixture, and stir until incorporated.

6. Stuff each mushroom cap with 1 tablespoon of the sausage mixture, making a small mound on the top. Place on a baking sheet, and bake for 25 minutes or until the mushrooms are slightly brown on the top. Season with salt and black pepper, and serve.

THAI GLAZED CHICKEN WINGS

| SERVES 6 |

Drizzled with a flavorful and sweet Thai glaze, these wings are the perfect appetizer for any party, get-together, or game day!

PREP TIME	COOK TIME	TOTAL TIME
5 minutes	*50 minutes*	*55 minutes*

1. Preheat the oven to 400°F (205°C). Line a baking sheet with parchment paper or foil, and lightly coat with cooking spray.

2. Pat dry the wings with a paper towel, and add the wings to a zipper-lock bag. Add the baking powder, salt, and black pepper, and shake to coat evenly. Place the wings on the prepared baking sheet.

3. Bake for 45 to 50 minutes or until crispy and no longer pink. Remove from the oven.

4. Right before the wings are done, make the Thai glaze. In a medium saucepan over medium-high heat, combine the Thai sweet chili sauce, brown sugar, soy sauce, rice wine vinegar, garlic, sesame oil, and lime juice. Bring to a boil and then reduce the heat to low and simmer for 2 or 3 minutes.

5. Switch the oven to the broiler setting.

6. Brush half of the glaze on the cooked wings, and broil the wings for 2 or 3 minutes or until the glaze caramelizes.

7. Brush the remaining glaze on top of the finished wings. Garnish with peanuts and parsley, if using, and serve.

4 lb (2kg) chicken wings

1 tbsp baking powder

1 tsp salt

¼ tsp freshly ground black pepper

Chopped peanuts, for garnish (optional)

Chopped fresh parsley, for garnish (optional)

FOR THE THAI GLAZE

¾ cup Thai sweet chili sauce

¼ cup packed brown sugar

¼ cup soy sauce

2 tbsp rice wine vinegar

3 cloves garlic, minced

1 tsp sesame oil

Juice of ½ lime

To view on device

JALAPEÑO BACON CHEESEBALL

| SERVES 12 |

No get-together is complete without a cheeseball. This creamy and flavorful appetizer combines the heat of jalapeños, the saltiness of bacon, and the crunch of pecans. It's easy to make and will impress your guests at any gathering.

PREP TIME
15 minutes + 1 hour to cool and set

COOK TIME
None

TOTAL TIME
1 hour 15 minutes

16oz (450g) cream cheese, softened

3 fresh jalapeños, seeded and finely chopped

1 cup shredded cheddar cheese

8 slices bacon, crisp-cooked, drained, and chopped

¼ cup chopped green onions

1 tsp seasoning salt

1 tsp minced garlic

1 tsp Worcestershire sauce

¼ tsp ground cumin

½ cup coarsely chopped pecans

Crackers, your choice, for serving

1. In a medium bowl, stir together the cream cheese, half of the jalapeños, cheddar cheese, half of the bacon, green onions, seasoning salt, garlic, Worcestershire sauce, and cumin.

2. On a large plate, combine the remaining halves of the jalapeños and bacon with the pecans.

3. Shape the cream cheese mixture into a ball, and roll it in the jalapeños, bacon, and pecans on the plate until fully coated.

4. Wrap the cheeseball in plastic wrap, and chill for 1 hour before serving with your choice of crackers. Store any leftovers in an airtight container in the refrigerator for up to 4 days.

To view on device

OLIVE OIL BREAD DIP

| SERVES 6 |

This easy and delicious bread dip is the perfect appetizer for parties or any type of gathering.
I like to add it to a charcuterie board. I love using it with any French bread or crostini.

PREP TIME
5 minutes

COOK TIME
None

TOTAL TIME
5 minutes

1 cup extra-virgin olive oil

3 cloves garlic, minced

½ tbsp **Easy Italian Seasoning** (page 263)

1 tsp chopped fresh parsley

½ tsp crushed red pepper flakes

Salt and freshly ground black pepper

1. In a small bowl, combine the extra-virgin olive oil, garlic, Easy Italian Seasoning, parsley, and crushed red pepper flakes.

2. Season with salt and black pepper, and serve.

To view on device

EASY AVOCADO SALSA

| SERVES 4 |

A fiesta in a bowl! With creamy avocados, zesty tomatoes, a kick of jalapeño, and a burst of lime, every bite is delicious. Grab your tortilla chips, and dive into this delicious dip everyone will love.

PREP TIME	COOK TIME	TOTAL TIME
10 minutes	*None*	*10 minutes*

4 avocados, pitted and diced

5 Roma tomatoes, diced

½ red onion, diced

1 fresh jalapeño, diced

½ cup chopped fresh cilantro

Juice of 1 lime

3 cloves garlic, minced

½ tsp salt

¼ tsp freshly ground black pepper

1. In a medium bowl, combine the avocados, Roma tomatoes, red onion, jalapeño, cilantro, lime juice, garlic, salt, and black pepper.

2. Serve immediately with tortilla chips.

To view on device

JALAPEÑO POPPERS WITH BACON

| SERVES 12–15 |

These jalapeños poppers are filled with a cream cheese mixture that's packed
with bacon. They're the perfect handheld appetizer that can be served for
any occasion. Fair warning: you won't be able to stop at just one!

PREP TIME	COOK TIME	TOTAL TIME
10 minutes	*20 minutes*	*30 minutes*

10 large jalapeños

8oz (225g) cream cheese, softened

½ tsp garlic powder

½ tsp salt

¼ tsp freshly ground black pepper

1½ cups shredded cheddar cheese

½ lb (225g) bacon, crisp-cooked, drained, and crumbled

¼ cup sliced green onions

1. Preheat the oven to 400°F (205°C).

2. Wearing gloves, slice each jalapeño in half lengthwise and use a spoon to remove the ribs and seeds.

3. In a medium bowl, combine the cream cheese, garlic powder, salt, black pepper, cheddar cheese, bacon, and green onions.

4. Evenly divide the cream cheese mixture among the jalapeños, and place the filled peppers on a baking sheet. Bake for 20 minutes or until the jalapeños are tender. Serve hot.

To view on device

PEACH CROSTINI
with Creamy Feta and Prosciutto

| SERVES 6 |

This crostini is a delightful combination of crispy baguette slices, creamy whipped feta, sweet peach slices, savory prosciutto, and a touch of basil and pistachios, all brought together with a drizzle of balsamic glaze. The result is a mouthwatering appetizer that perfectly balances flavors and textures.

PREP TIME
10 minutes

COOK TIME
15 minutes

TOTAL TIME
25 minutes

1 baguette, cut into ½-in (1.25cm) slices

3 tbsp olive oil, divided

½ tsp sea salt

6oz (170g) feta cheese, crumbled

2oz (55g) cream cheese

3 tbsp extra-virgin olive oil, plus more if needed

1 tsp garlic, minced

Salt and freshly ground black pepper

4oz (115g) prosciutto

3 small peaches, thinly sliced

Chopped fresh basil

2 tbsp chopped pistachios

Balsamic glaze, for drizzle

1. Preheat the oven to 400°F (205°C).

2. Lay the baguette slices on a baking sheet. Drizzle 1½ tablespoons olive oil over the top, and sprinkle with sea salt.

3. Bake for 7 to 10 minutes, flip over the slices, and drizzle the other side with 1½ tablespoons olive oil. Bake for 3 to 5 more minutes or until crispy and browned.

4. Meanwhile, in a food processor, pulse together the feta cheese, cream cheese, extra-virgin olive oil, garlic, salt, and black pepper until smooth and creamy. Add more extra-virgin olive oil if needed to blend.

5. Spread a layer of the whipped feta on each slice of the toasted bread. Add a layer of prosciutto, followed by a few peach slices. Top with fresh basil and pistachios, drizzle with balsamic glaze, and serve.

INSANELY DELICIOUS HOT CRAB DIP

| SERVES 12 |

Ready in less than 30 minutes, this deliciously cheesy warm dip makes
the perfect party appetizer. I like to dip into it with a crusty bread or cracker
(veggies are great, too), and once I start, I can't stop.

PREP TIME
5 minutes

COOK TIME
20 minutes

TOTAL TIME
25 minutes

8oz (225g) cream cheese, softened

¼ cup sour cream

¼ cup mayonnaise

1 cup grated cheddar cheese

1 tsp garlic powder

½ tsp sweet paprika

1 tbsp Worcestershire sauce

1 tbsp lemon juice

½ tsp salt

¼ tsp freshly ground black pepper

1 lb (450g) canned lump crabmeat

Sliced green onions, for garnish

1. Preheat the oven to 350°F (175°C).

2. In a medium bowl, combine the cream cheese, sour cream, mayonnaise, cheddar cheese, garlic powder, sweet paprika, Worcestershire sauce, lemon juice, salt, and black pepper.

3. Fold in the lump crabmeat.

4. Spread the dip in a small casserole dish, and bake for 20 to 25 minutes or until heated through and bubbly. Garnish with green onions, and serve with baguette slices, tortilla chips, or fresh vegetables.

To view on device

HUMMUS FLATBREAD
with Arugula and Veggies

COOKBOOK EXCLUSIVE

| SERVES 2 |

Fresh, full of flavor, and packed with healthy ingredients, this hummus flatbread can be served as an appetizer or a delicious lunch. Grilling the flatbread is optional, but it gives the bread a nice char and smokiness that really elevates the flavor.

PREP TIME
15 minutes

COOK TIME
5 minutes

TOTAL TIME
20 minutes

1 large naan flatbread

½ cup halved multicolored cherry tomatoes

¼ cup sliced cucumber

¼ cup pitted Kalamata olives

2 tbsp diced red onion

¼ cup canned chickpeas (garbanzo beans), rinsed and drained

¼ cup arugula

Juice of ½ lemon

½ cup hummus

2 tbsp crumbled feta cheese

Salt and freshly ground black pepper

Drizzle of extra-virgin olive oil

1. Preheat the grill to medium-high.

2. Grill the naan flatbread for 2 or 3 minutes per side until it's browned and has a slight char. Remove from the grill.

3. In a medium bowl, combine the cherry tomatoes, cucumber, Kalamata olives, red onion, chickpeas, and arugula. Squeeze the lemon juice over the top, and toss to coat.

4. Spread the hummus on the flatbread. Top with the vegetable mixture. Sprinkle the feta over the vegetables. Season with salt and black pepper, drizzle with extra-virgin olive oil, and serve.

BACON-WRAPPED WATER CHESTNUTS

| SERVES 24 |

These sweet and crunchy water chestnuts are caramelized in a sauce made
with brown sugar and then wrapped in savory bacon. They make the best
finger-food appetizer, and I love serving them at parties.

PREP TIME
15 minutes + 2 hours to marinate

COOK TIME
45 minutes

TOTAL TIME
3 hours

1 lb (450g) bacon, or turkey bacon,
cut in half

2 (8oz/225g) cans whole water
chestnuts, drained

¼ cup packed brown sugar

¼ cup sweet chili sauce

½ cup mayonnaise

To view on device

1. Wrap 1 half-strip of bacon around each water chestnut, and skewer with
   a toothpick to hold the bacon in place. Place the bacon-wrapped
   chestnuts in a 9×13-inch (23×33cm) baking pan.

2. In a small bowl, combine the brown sugar, sweet chili sauce, and
   mayonnaise. Pour the sauce over the chestnuts.

3. Place in the refrigerator, and marinate for 2 hours.

4. Preheat the oven to 350°F (175°C).

5. Bake for 45 minutes. During the last 5 minutes, turn on the broiler to
   crisp the bacon. These are best served warm. Store any leftovers in an
   airtight container in the refrigerator for up to 4 days. To reheat, place on
   a baking sheet in a 350°F (175°C) oven for about 15 minutes or until
   warmed through.

HOT HAM AND SWISS PINWHEELS

| SERVES 14 |

These pinwheels are rolled to ensure you get a taste of
salty ham and creamy cheese in every bite. My favorite part
is the poppy seed topping that's brushed on with melted butter.
These pinwheels make a great quick and easy dinner option,
or they can be served as an appetizer at any gathering.

PREP TIME	COOK TIME	TOTAL TIME
10 minutes	*15 minutes*	*25 minutes*

1 (8oz/225g) tube crescent roll dough

4 tsp Dijon mustard

8oz (225g) sliced Swiss cheese

½ lb (225g) sliced deli ham

¼ cup unsalted butter, melted

½ tbsp Worcestershire sauce

¼ tsp garlic powder

2 tbsp minced fresh parsley

1 tsp poppy seeds

1. Preheat the oven to 350°F (175°C). Lightly coat an 8×8-inch
   (20×20cm) baking pan with cooking spray.

2. Unroll the croissant dough, pinch the seams to seal, and divide the
   dough into 4 sections.

3. Spread about 1 heaping teaspoon Dijon mustard over each section.
   Add 2 slices each of Swiss cheese and ham over the mustard. Roll
   up each rectangle, and seal the seam.

4. Cut each roll into 3 or 4 slices, and place them in the prepared
   baking pan.

5. In a small bowl, combine the melted butter, Worcestershire sauce,
   garlic powder, parsley, and poppy seeds. Using a pastry brush,
   brush the mixture on top of the pinwheels.

6. Bake for 13 to 15 minutes or until golden brown. Serve warm or at
   room temperature. Store any leftovers in an airtight container in the
   refrigerator for up to 4 days. Reheat in a 375°F (190°C) oven for
   5 to 10 minutes or until warmed through.

To view on device

5-Minute
MILLION-DOLLAR DIP

| SERVES 12 |

*I can't tell you how much I love this dip! It's a hit at every barbecue, potluck,
and game day around our house, and we never host an event without it.
It's so easy and delicious—it's not called "million-dollar dip" for nothing!*

PREP TIME
5 minutes + 2 hours to chill

COOK TIME
None

TOTAL TIME
2 hours 5 minutes

5 green onions, chopped

1 cup shredded cheddar cheese

1½ cups mayonnaise

½ cup real bacon bits

½ cup slivered almonds

1. In a medium bowl, combine the green onions, cheddar cheese, mayonnaise, bacon bits, and almonds.

2. Cover and chill for at least 2 hours.

3. Serve with your favorite crackers.

To view on device

2 cups all-purpose flour

2 tbsp cornstarch

½ tsp salt

¼ tsp freshly ground black pepper

Pinch of crushed red pepper flakes
(optional)

3 cups 1% milk

Vegetable oil, for frying

1 head cauliflower, cut into florets

Sliced green onion, for garnish

White and black sesame seeds, for garnish

FOR THE HONEY GARLIC SAUCE

½ cup honey

¼ cup soy sauce

3 cloves garlic, minced

Juice of ½ lemon

2 tbsp cornstarch

1 tbsp cold water

Sticky Honey Garlic
FRIED CAULIFLOWER

| SERVES 6 |

This tasty appetizer will appeal to just about anyone. The cauliflower is fried and then drenched in a honey garlic sauce that is bursting with flavor. I like to double the recipe because no one can resist this starter.

PREP TIME	COOK TIME	TOTAL TIME
10 minutes	*15 minutes*	*25 minutes*

1. In a medium bowl, combine the all-purpose flour, cornstarch, salt, black pepper, and crushed red pepper flakes. Add the milk, and mix until combined.

2. In a large pot, add enough vegetable oil to come about 3 inches (7.5cm) up the side. Set over medium-high heat, and heat the oil to about 350°F (175°C). (You can use a deep fryer instead, if you like.)

3. Spear each cauliflower floret onto a fork, dip into the batter, and shake to remove any excess batter. Place on a parchment paper–lined baking sheet. Repeat with the remaining cauliflower.

4. Using tongs, add the battered florets to the hot oil, and fry for about 4 minutes or until golden brown. Using a slotted spoon, transfer to a paper towel–lined plate.

5. In a small saucepan over medium-high heat, combine the honey, soy sauce, garlic, and lemon juice, and cook for 2 minutes.

6. In a small bowl, whisk together the cornstarch and cold water. Pour the cornstarch mixture into the honey garlic sauce, and whisk for about 2 or 3 minutes or until the sauce thickens.

7. Pour the sauce over the cooked cauliflower, and toss to coat. Garnish with green onions and white and black sesame seeds, and serve.

DELICIOUS AVOCADO EGG ROLLS

| SERVES 4 |

These tasty egg rolls are crispy on the outside with an avocado mixture inside
that is bursting with flavor. I love these best when they are dipped in ranch
or cilantro lime dressing, but they are wonderful plain, too.

PREP TIME
15 minutes

COOK TIME
5 minutes

TOTAL TIME
20 minutes

1 cup vegetable oil, for frying

3 avocados, pitted and diced

¼ cup diced red onion

1 Roma tomato, diced

3 tbsp chopped fresh cilantro leaves

1 tsp garlic powder

Juice of 1 lime

Salt and freshly ground black pepper

8 egg roll wrappers

1. In a large skillet over medium-high heat, heat the vegetable oil.

2. In a medium bowl, mash the avocados to your desired consistency. Add the red onion, Roma tomato, cilantro, garlic powder, lime juice, salt, and black pepper to taste.

3. Spoon 1 or 2 tablespoons avocado mixture in the center of an egg roll wrapper. Using your finger, rub the edges of the wrapper with water. Roll the bottom edge of the wrapper tightly over the filling. Fold in the sides, roll up the wrapper, and press to seal. Repeat with the remaining wrappers.

4. Add the egg rolls to the hot oil in batches, and fry for 2 or 3 minutes or until golden brown on all sides. Using metal tongs, remove the cooked egg rolls to a paper towel–lined plate. Serve immediately, plain or with your favorite dipping sauce.

NOTE

You can cook these quickly, and with less mess, in an air fryer. Place the egg rolls in the basket, lightly spray the tops with cooking spray, and cook at 400°F (205°C) for 6 minutes. Flip over the egg rolls, and cook for 6 more minutes.

To view on device

ARANCINI
with Pancetta and Peas

| SERVES 4 |

These deep-fried rice balls are an Italian finger food. Filled with cheese and coated with Italian breadcrumbs, they offer a delicious flavor and combination of spices. I like to dip them in my **Family Favorite Alfredo Sauce** (page 202) or **Homemade Marinara Sauce** (page 263).

PREP TIME
*10 minutes +
30 minutes to chill*

COOK TIME
30 minutes

TOTAL TIME
1 hour 10 minutes

2 tbsp unsalted butter

1 small white onion, finely chopped

3 cloves garlic, finely chopped

½ cup chopped pancetta

½ cup dry white wine

1 cup uncooked arborio rice

2½ cups chicken broth

½ cup frozen peas, thawed

2 tbsp finely chopped fresh parsley

½ tsp salt

¼ tsp freshly ground black pepper

½ cup freshly shredded Romano or
   Parmesan cheese

4oz (115g) fresh mozzarella,
   cut into ½-in (1.25cm) cubes

2 cups all-purpose flour

3 eggs, whisked

2 cups Italian breadcrumbs

Vegetable oil, for frying

1. In a large saucepan or Dutch oven with a tight-fitting lid over medium-high heat, melt the butter. Add the white onion, and sauté for about 3 or 4 minutes. Add the garlic and pancetta, and sauté for 1 or 2 minutes until the prosciutto turns lightly brown.

2. Pour in the white wine, and stir until the liquid evaporates. Add the rice and chicken broth, 1 cup of broth at a time. Cover and simmer for about 15 to 20 minutes or until the rice has absorbed the liquid.

3. Stir in the thawed peas, parsley, salt, and black pepper. Remove the mixture from the heat and transfer to a bowl to cool completely.

4. When cool, stir in the Romano or Parmesan cheese.

5. Using a ladle, scoop about ½ cup of the rice mixture, and shape it into a ball with wet hands. Flatten it slightly, and create an indentation. Stuff the center with 1 mozzarella cheese cube. Roll the rice back into a ball, and place on a parchment paper–lined baking sheet. Repeat with the remaining rice.

6. Create a dredging station by placing the all-purpose flour, eggs, and Italian breadcrumbs each into three separate small bowls. Dip the rice balls into the flour and coat completely. Then coat in egg, using a fork to allow the excess egg to shake off. Dredge in the breadcrumbs next, coating completely. Lay the coated balls on a plate, and repeat with the remaining balls.

7. Place in the refrigerator, and chill for 30 minutes.

8. In a heavy-bottomed Dutch oven over medium-high heat, heat the vegetable oil to 350°F (175°C). Using a slotted spoon, lower the rice balls into the hot oil, and fry for about 2 or 3 minutes or until golden. Transfer to a paper towel–lined plate and repeat with the remaining balls. Serve hot.

HOT SPINACH ARTICHOKE DIP

| SERVES 10 |

This dip is a mouthwatering combination of creamy cheeses, flavorful garlic, and hearty vegetables. With its warm and bubbly texture, it's the perfect appetizer to impress your guests or enjoy as a scrumptious snack.

PREP TIME
10 minutes

COOK TIME
20 minutes

TOTAL TIME
30 minutes

8oz (225g) cream cheese, softened

½ cup sour cream

¼ cup mayonnaise

3 cloves garlic, minced

½ cup shredded mozzarella cheese

1 cup grated Parmesan cheese

1 (14oz/400g) can artichokes, drained and chopped

6oz (170g) frozen spinach, thawed

1. Preheat the oven to 400°F (205°C).

2. In a medium bowl, combine the cream cheese, sour cream, and mayonnaise.

3. Add the garlic, mozzarella cheese, Parmesan cheese, artichokes, and spinach, and stir well to combine.

4. Evenly spread the mixture into a 1-quart (1-liter) baking dish, and bake for 15 to 20 minutes or until heated through and bubbly. Serve warm with a sliced baguette or crackers.

To view on device

SUSHI NACHOS

| SERVES 8 |

Nachos are always a crowd-pleaser, with salty, crunchy chips and endless toppings. But make them into *sushi nachos*, and you have just taken this favorite appetizer to the next level! A wonton chip base is topped with crab, tuna, and veggies and then drizzled with my favorite spicy sriracha mayo and eel sauce—my mouth waters just thinking about them!

PREP TIME	COOK TIME	TOTAL TIME
20 minutes	*None*	*20 minutes*

4 cups wonton chips

½ cup chopped imitation crab

½ cup chopped ahi tuna

¼ cup chopped cucumber

1 fresh jalapeño, chopped (Remove the seeds if you don't want any heat.)

1 avocado, pitted and chopped

Spicy Sriracha Mayo (page 262), to taste

Eel sauce, to taste

Cilantro lime sauce, to taste

Chopped fresh cilantro, for garnish

Sliced green onions, for garnish

Sesame seeds, for garnish

Crushed nori, for garnish

1. Layer the wonton chips on a plate, and top with the imitation crab, ahi tuna, cucumbers, jalapeño, and avocado.

2. Over the top, drizzle the Spicy Sriracha Mayo, eel sauce, and cilantro lime sauce. Garnish with cilantro, green onions, sesame seeds, and crushed nori, and serve immediately.

NOTE

If you want to make your own wonton chips, here's how, using wonton wrappers:

1. Fill a large, heavy-bottomed pot ½ to ⅔ of the way full with your preferred frying oil. Heat the oil to 360°F (185°C). Use an oil or candy thermometer to monitor the temperature while frying, adjusting the heat to keep the oil between 350°F and 360°F (175–185°C).

2. Cut the wonton wrappers into triangles, and cover the uncooked wrappers with a clean kitchen towel between batches. Add 6 or 7 triangles (or more if your pot is large enough) to the oil at a time, and fry for 60 to 90 seconds or until puffed and deep golden brown, using a spider or slotted spoon to separate the chips from each other as they fry. Don't overcrowd the pot as you fry or the temperature of the oil will drop and the chips will be oily.

3. Using a spider or slotted spoon, transfer the golden brown chips to a paper towel–lined baking sheet, and cool completely before serving.

WHIPPED FETA DIP

| SERVES 8 |

Dips are the perfect thing to serve at a party, and this whipped feta is no exception.
The combination of feta cheese mixed with garlic, lemon zest, and crushed red
pepper flakes makes a dip with just the right amount of flavor. I like to serve
it with some pita bread, crostini, crackers, carrots, or cucumbers.

PREP TIME	COOK TIME	TOTAL TIME
10 minutes	*None*	*10 minutes*

12oz (340g) feta cheese (crumbled or block)

8oz (225g) cream cheese, softened

1 clove garlic

2 tbsp extra-virgin olive oil, plus more for garnish

Zest of ½ lemon (about ½ tbsp)

Juice of ½ lemon (about 1 tbsp)

½ tsp salt

¼ tsp freshly ground black pepper

Pinch of crushed red pepper flakes

Chopped fresh parsley, for garnish

1. In a food processor, pulse together the feta cheese, cream cheese, garlic, extra-virgin olive oil, lemon zest, lemon juice, salt, black pepper, and crushed red pepper flakes until smooth and creamy.

2. Transfer to a serving bowl, drizzle with olive oil, garnish with parsley, and serve with your choice of dippers.

To view on device

SIDE DISHES

Scrumptious side dishes elevate your meals to the next level. Whether you prefer creamy flavors or crave crispy textures, there's something for everyone in this section. Discover my top picks, like the **Easy Vegetable Stir-Fry** (page 152) and the flavorful **Parmesan Garlic Roasted Potatoes** (page 139). Looking for a comforting baked option? The **Stick of Butter Baked Rice** (page 142) is a family favorite that never disappoints. If you love grilling, don't miss out on the must-try **Grilled Mexican Street Corn** (page 144) and the amazing goodness of the **Caramelized Grilled Pineapple** (page 151). These recipes are guaranteed to make your side dishes shine as the true stars at your dinner table.

◄ *Dare I say that some of my side dishes have actually become the stars of the show? These sides are some of my top recipes and the most requested from my family every year.*

CREAMY PARMESAN GARLIC BRUSSELS SPROUTS

| SERVES 6 |

Sautéed brussels sprouts are tossed in a velvety blend of chicken broth, heavy cream, and Parmesan cheese, creating a rich and flavorful side dish that's perfectly seasoned with garlic and Italian herbs.

PREP TIME
5 minutes

COOK TIME
15 minutes

TOTAL TIME
20 minutes

1½ lb (680g) brussels sprouts, halved

3 cloves garlic, minced

1 tbsp olive oil

½ cup chicken broth

½ cup heavy cream

2 tsp cornstarch

½ cup grated Parmesan cheese

1 tsp **Easy Italian Seasoning**
(page 263)

Salt and freshly ground black pepper

1. In a medium skillet over medium heat, sauté the brussels sprouts and garlic in the olive oil for 5 to 7 minutes or until almost tender. Remove the brussels sprouts from the skillet, and set aside.

2. Add the chicken broth, heavy cream, and cornstarch, and whisk until smooth. Add the Parmesan cheese, Easy Italian Seasoning, salt, and black pepper, and simmer for 5 to 7 minutes or until the sauce starts to thicken.

3. Return the brussels sprouts to the skillet, toss to coat in the sauce, and cook for 3 or 4 minutes or until heated through. Serve hot.

To view on device

ROASTED PARMESAN GARLIC ZUCCHINI SPEARS

| SERVES 4 |

When your garden is ripe with zucchini, this is the perfect recipe to make the most of it. These zucchini spears are coated with Parmesan cheese and garlic, seasoned to perfection, and roasted. They're an easy side that will complement any meal.

PREP TIME
10 minutes

COOK TIME
15 minutes

TOTAL TIME
25 minutes

3 medium zucchini (about 1½ lb/680g)

Salt and freshly ground black pepper

1 tbsp olive oil

2 tsp lemon zest

1 tbsp lemon juice

1 clove garlic, minced

½ tsp ground oregano

3 tbsp grated Parmesan cheese

To view on device

1. Preheat the oven to 350°F (175°C). Line a baking sheet with foil, and lightly coat the foil with cooking spray.

2. Cut the zucchini lengthwise into quarters and then cut each quarter in half. Lay the zucchini spears on the prepared baking sheet, and sprinkle with salt and black pepper.

3. In a small bowl, whisk together the olive oil, lemon zest, lemon juice, garlic, and oregano. Drizzle over the zucchini spears and then sprinkle with the Parmesan cheese.

4. Bake for 15 minutes or until lightly golden brown. To give the spears crisp edges, broil for the last 3 minutes. Serve hot.

PARMESAN GARLIC ROASTED POTATOES

| SERVES 6–8 |

The perfect side dish for any occasion, these red potatoes are roasted to perfection. They have a crispy edge, made with freshly grated Parmesan cheese; the inside is so tender, it melts in your mouth; and the roasted garlic adds mouthwatering flavor.

PREP TIME	COOK TIME	TOTAL TIME
10 minutes	*35 minutes*	*45 minutes*

1. Preheat the oven to 400°F (205°C). Lightly spray a baking sheet with cooking spray.

2. In a large bowl, combine the olive oil, Parmesan cheese, garlic, oregano, and potatoes, until the potatoes are completely coated.

3. Arrange the potatoes in a single layer on the prepared baking sheet. Season with salt and black pepper. (I like to sprinkle some additional Parmesan over the top.)

4. Roast for 30 to 35 minutes or until golden brown and crisp. Garnish with parsley and rosemary, and serve.

2 tbsp olive oil

½ cup grated Parmesan cheese

3 cloves garlic, minced

½ tsp dried oregano

2 lb (1kg) red potatoes, skin on, cut into 1-in (2.5cm) pieces

¼ tsp salt

¼ tsp freshly ground black pepper

Chopped fresh parsley, for garnish

Rosemary sprigs, cut into 1-in (2.5cm) pieces, for garnish

To view on device

EASY FRIED RICE

| SERVES 8 |

You know when you want takeout but it's just not an option? This recipe is going to be your new favorite because it is *better* than takeout! It's filled with all the delicious vegetables and flavors from your favorite restaurant, but you can make it at home any time you want.

PREP TIME	COOK TIME	TOTAL TIME
15 minutes	*15 minutes*	*30 minutes*

2 tbsp sesame oil

1 small white onion, chopped

1 cup frozen peas and carrots, thawed

2 eggs, lightly beaten

3 cups cooked rice (I like to use long-grain or jasmine rice.)

2–3 tbsp reduced-sodium soy sauce, or to taste

2 tbsp chopped green onions (optional)

1. Preheat a large skillet or wok over medium heat. Add the sesame oil, white onion, and peas and carrots, and cook for 3 or 4 minutes or until tender.

2. Slide the cooked vegetables to the side of the skillet, and pour the eggs onto the other side. Using a spatula, scramble the eggs. After the eggs are cooked, mix them with the vegetables.

3. Add the rice to the skillet, and pour the soy sauce over the top. Stir and fry the rice and veggie mixture for 5 minutes or until warmed through and well combined.

4. Add the green onions, if using, and serve.

NOTE

Leftover cooked rice makes the best fried rice. Using cold day-old rice for this recipe prevents the rice from being mushy and tastes just like takeout.

To view on device

STICK OF BUTTER BAKED RICE

| SERVES 8 |

In this classic side dish, rice is cooked in beef broth, French onion soup, and a stick of butter and absorbs all those delicious flavors. The end result is soft and fluffy rice that is baked to perfection.

PREP TIME
5 minutes

COOK TIME
1 hour

TOTAL TIME
1 hour 5 minutes

1 cup uncooked long-grain rice (not instant)

1 (14oz/400g) can French onion soup (Campbell's recommended)

1 (14oz/400g) can beef broth

½ cup unsalted butter, sliced

1. Preheat the oven to 425°F (220°C).

2. Add the long-grain rice, French onion soup, beef broth, and butter to an 8×8-inch (20×20cm) casserole dish. Cover with foil, and bake for 30 minutes.

3. Remove the foil, and bake for 30 more minutes.

4. Remove from the oven, fluff with a fork, and serve.

To view on device

CHEESY ZUCCHINI GRATIN

| SERVES 6 |

This delicious veggie side is sure to please any crowd. Zucchini slices are layered with a creamy, cheesy sauce and cooked until golden brown— this dish is as beautiful as it is delicious. It's an ooey-gooey, low-carb take on comfort food that goes with any meal.

PREP TIME	COOK TIME	TOTAL TIME
15 minutes	*30 minutes*	*45 minutes*

2 tbsp unsalted butter

2 tbsp all-purpose flour

1 tsp salt

½ tsp freshly ground black pepper

2 cups heavy whipping cream or half-and-half

½ cup shredded Parmesan cheese

6 small zucchini, sliced about ¼ inch (0.5cm) thick

1 cup shredded mozzarella cheese

½ cup shredded Gruyère cheese

Minced fresh chives, for garnish

1. Preheat the oven to 400°F (205°C). Lightly spray a 2-quart casserole dish with cooking spray.

2. In a small saucepan over medium heat, melt the butter. Add the flour, salt, and black pepper, and stir.

3. Add the heavy whipping cream, and stir for about 2 minutes or until the sauce starts to thicken.

4. Add ¼ cup Parmesan cheese.

5. Arrange half of the zucchini slices in the prepared casserole dish, overlapping each other. Spread half of the sauce on top, followed by ½ of the mozzarella cheese and all of the Gruyère cheese. Repeat with another layer of the remaining zucchini and sauce topped with the remaining mozzarella and remaining ¼ cup Parmesan.

6. Bake for about 25 minutes or until the zucchini is fork-tender and the top starts to brown. Garnish with chives, and serve.

To view on device

GRILLED MEXICAN STREET CORN

| SERVES 4 |

This grilled side dish is perfect for any barbecue or outdoor gathering. The corn is slathered with a fantastic mayonnaise blend and topped with Parmesan cheese and chili powder. It has just the right amount of flavor but doesn't pack too much heat. Even my kids love it!

PREP TIME	COOK TIME	TOTAL TIME
10 minutes	*15 minutes*	*25 minutes*

1. Preheat a grill to medium, or heat a cast-iron skillet over medium heat. Add the corn, and grill for about 2 or 3 minutes per side or until it starts to get slightly charred.

2. In a small bowl, combine the mayonnaise, sour cream, and cilantro.

3. Remove the corn from the grill, slather it with the mayonnaise mixture using a basting brush, and set on a serving platter.

4. Squeeze the lime juice over the corn, and sprinkle it generously with Parmesan cheese and cotija cheese. Sprinkle with chili powder to taste (sprinkle generously if you like a lot of heat), and serve with lime wedges.

4 ears corn, husks removed

3 tbsp mayonnaise

½ cup sour cream

¼ cup chopped fresh cilantro

Juice of 1 lime (about 2 tbsp)

½ cup freshly grated Parmesan cheese

¼ cup cotija cheese

Chili powder

2 limes, cut into wedges, to serve

To view on device

GARLIC PARMESAN GREEN BEANS
with Bacon

| SERVES 12 |

I love a side dish that combines bacon with veggies. These green beans have so much flavor, they go perfectly with any entrée. I also love any chance I get to use fresh vegetables from my garden, and this dish is the perfect recipe for fresh green beans.

PREP TIME	COOK TIME	TOTAL TIME
10 minutes	*20 minutes*	*30 minutes*

2 lb (1kg) green beans

½ lb (225g) bacon, diced

1 tbsp unsalted butter

3 cloves garlic, minced

3 tbsp grated Parmesan cheese

Salt and freshly ground black pepper

1. Trim the ends off the green beans, and slice them into 2-inch (5cm) pieces.

2. Bring a large pot of water to a boil over medium-high heat, and add the green beans. Cook for about 5 to 7 minutes or until tender. Drain and transfer the green beans to an ice bath.

3. In a medium skillet over medium-high heat, cook the bacon for 3 or 4 minutes or until crisp. Remove from the skillet using a slotted spoon, and drain and discard the fat.

4. Add the butter to the skillet. Add the garlic, and sauté for 4 to 6 minutes or until tender.

5. Add the bacon, green beans, and Parmesan cheese, and cook for 2 or 3 minutes or until heated through. Season with salt and black pepper, and serve.

To view on device

ROASTED BROWN BUTTER HONEY GARLIC CARROTS

| SERVES 6 |

These sweet and flavorful carrots are the perfect side dish to complement any meal. They are roasted to perfection in a delicious sauce that makes them tender on the inside and golden brown on the outside. My family devours these every time I make them. They will elevate any meal.

PREP TIME
5 minutes

COOK TIME
25 minutes

TOTAL TIME
30 minutes

½ cup unsalted butter

3 tbsp honey

2 cloves garlic, chopped

2 lb (1kg) large carrots, peeled and cut into 2-in (5cm) pieces

Salt and freshly ground black pepper

Chopped fresh parsley, for garnish

1. Preheat the oven to 425°F (220°C).

2. In a medium saucepan over medium-high heat, heat the butter. Cook, whisking continuously, for 3 or 4 minutes or until the butter begins to become frothy and brown.

3. When the butter is browned, add the honey and garlic, stir, and then remove the pan from the heat.

4. Add the carrots to a large bowl, drizzle the sauce over the top, and toss until evenly coated. Spread the carrots in a single layer on a large baking sheet. Lightly season with salt and black pepper.

5. Cover the baking sheet with foil. Bake the carrots for 10 minutes. Remove the foil, and bake for 5 to 10 more minutes or until the carrots are browned and tender.

6. Transfer to a serving dish, sprinkle the chopped parsley over the top, and serve immediately.

NOTE

Baby carrots also will work. Reduce the cook time to about 10 or 15 minutes because they are smaller and cook faster.

To view on device

5-INGREDIENT CORN CASSEROLE

| SERVES 8 |

This side dish is simple (takes just 5 minutes to prepare) and so delicious. It's a favorite of ours, especially around the holidays, and you won't see us celebrate Thanksgiving without it!

PREP TIME
5 minutes

COOK TIME
55 minutes

TOTAL TIME
1 hour

1 (8oz/225g) box corn muffin mix

1 (15oz/425g) can whole kernel corn, drained

1 (15oz/425g) can creamed corn, with liquid

1 cup sour cream

½ cup unsalted butter, melted

Chopped green onions, for garnish

1. Preheat the oven to 350°F (175°C). Lightly coat an 8×8-inch (20×20cm) baking pan with cooking spray.

2. In a large bowl, stir together the corn muffin mix, whole kernel corn, creamed corn with liquid, sour cream, and butter until combined. Pour into the prepared baking pan.

3. Bake uncovered for 45 to 55 minutes or until lightly browned. Garnish with green onions, and serve warm.

To view on device

2 medium russet potatoes, skin on

1 tbsp olive oil

1 tsp **Easy Italian Seasoning**
(page 263)

2 tbsp grated Parmesan cheese

½ tsp salt

¼ tsp freshly ground black pepper

AIR-FRYER FRENCH FRIES

| SERVES 4 |

These french fries taste like they're from a restaurant. They're perfectly crispy on the outside, tender on the inside, and go with just about any meal. I love that they are cooked in the air fryer, making them a healthy snack. Try dipping them in my homemade **Famous Fry Sauce** (page 264). The combination can't be beat!

PREP TIME	COOK TIME	TOTAL TIME
10 minutes	*20 minutes*	*30 minutes*

1. Preheat the air fryer to 380°F (195°C).

2. Slice the russet potatoes, using a fry cutter or a knife, into ¼-inch (0.5cm) strips.

3. Rinse the fries in cold water, and pat them dry with a paper towel.

4. In a medium bowl, toss the fries with the olive oil, Easy Italian Seasoning, Parmesan cheese, salt, and black pepper.

5. Place the fries in the air-fryer basket in a single layer. Cook for 15 to 20 minutes or until golden brown, tossing the fries halfway through the cook time to ensure they cook evenly.

NOTE

Don't skip rinsing the potatoes. This step is important because it gets rid of the starch, which allows the potatoes to get nice and crispy as they cook. Just be sure to dry them really well before cooking.

To view on device

CARAMELIZED GRILLED PINEAPPLE

| SERVES 6 |

Grilled is the best way to enjoy pineapple if you ask me. Covered in a cinnamon sauce that caramelizes as it heats, this pineapple is full of sweet flavor and turns out so incredibly juicy. It's a must for any barbecue.

PREP TIME
10 minutes

COOK TIME
10 minutes

TOTAL TIME
20 minutes

1 pineapple, cut into spears

½ cup unsalted butter, melted

½ cup packed brown sugar

1 tsp ground cinnamon, plus more for sprinkling

1. Preheat the grill to medium-high (about 400°F/205°C).

2. Place the pineapple spears on a lipped baking sheet, and sprinkle lightly with cinnamon.

3. In a small microwave-safe bowl, whisk together the butter, brown sugar, and 1 teaspoon cinnamon. If the sauce seems too thick, microwave it for a few seconds until it's more liquid. Using a pastry brush, spread the sauce on the pineapple.

4. Add the pineapple to the grill, and cook for about 3-4 minutes on each side or until it starts to turn golden brown.

5. Brush the pineapple with the excess sauce from the baking sheet, and serve.

To view on device

EASY VEGETABLE STIR-FRY

| SERVES 6 |

This quick and easy stir-fry is packed with flavor and color from some of my
favorite vegetables, but the sauce is the real star of the show. The delicious
glaze brings an amazing flavor that completes this veggie entrée.

PREP TIME
20 minutes

COOK TIME
5 minutes

TOTAL TIME
25 minutes

1 tbsp olive oil

1 red bell pepper, ribs and seeds
    removed, and sliced

1 yellow bell pepper, ribs and seeds
    removed, and sliced

1 cup sugar snap peas

1 cup sliced carrots

1 cup sliced button mushrooms

2 cups fresh broccoli florets

1 cup baby corn

½ cup water chestnuts

¼ cup soy sauce

3 cloves garlic, minced

3 tbsp brown sugar

1 tsp sesame oil

½ cup chicken broth or vegetable
    broth

1 tbsp cornstarch

Chopped green onions, for garnish
    (optional)

Sesame seeds, for garnish (optional)

1. In a wok or a large skillet over medium-high heat, heat the olive oil.
   Add the red bell pepper, yellow bell pepper, sugar snap peas, carrots,
   mushrooms, broccoli, baby corn, and water chestnuts, and sauté for
   2 or 3 minutes or until the veggies are almost tender.

2. In a small bowl, whisk together the soy sauce, garlic, brown sugar,
   sesame oil, chicken broth, and cornstarch.

3. Pour the cornstarch mixture over the veggies, and cook for 3 or
   4 minutes or until the sauce has thickened.

4. Garnish with green onions and sesame seeds, if using, and serve.

To view on device

CREAMY GARLIC PARMESAN MUSHROOMS

| SERVES 4 |

Calling all mushroom lovers! These creamy, cheesy, garlicky mushrooms are for you. Sautéed in garlic butter until tender and then tossed in the most *amazing* creamy Parmesan sauce, these easy mushrooms will be off the plate and in your mouth in just 10 minutes.

PREP TIME	COOK TIME	TOTAL TIME
5 minutes	*5 minutes*	*10 minutes*

1. In a medium skillet over medium-high heat, heat the butter and olive oil. Add the mushrooms and garlic, and sauté for 2 or 3 minutes or until tender.

2. Add the heavy cream, Parmesan cheese, cream cheese, Easy Italian Seasoning, salt, and black pepper. Stir to coat the mushrooms, and heat for 2 or 3 minutes or until the sauce is bubbly and smooth.

3. Garnish with fresh parsley, and serve.

2 tbsp unsalted butter

1 tbsp olive oil

8oz (225g) white mushrooms, whole or sliced

2 cloves garlic, minced

½ cup heavy cream

¼ cup grated Parmesan cheese

2oz (55g) cream cheese, softened

1 tsp **Easy Italian Seasoning** (page 263)

½ tsp salt

¼ tsp freshly ground black pepper

Chopped fresh parsley, for garnish

To view on device

ASIAN SLAW
with Spicy Cashew Dressing

COOKBOOK EXCLUSIVE

| SERVES 6 |

This colorful slaw is made with crisp, vibrant veggies and drizzled with a creamy cashew sauce. For an optional extra kick, sprinkle some crushed red pepper flakes over the top to add an extra punch of flavor.

PREP TIME	COOK TIME	TOTAL TIME
15 minutes	*None*	*15 minutes*

1. In a large bowl, add the green cabbage, purple cabbage, broccoli, carrots, edamame, red bell pepper, green onion, and cilantro.

2. In a medium bowl, make the dressing by whisking together the cashew butter, water, soy sauce, sriracha sauce, garlic, honey, sesame oil, rice vinegar, and salt. If needed, add a splash more water if the dressing is too thick to reach your desired consistency.

3. Drizzle the desired amount of dressing over the slaw, and toss to combine.

4. Garnish with chopped cashews, sesame seeds, and crushed red pepper flakes, if using, and serve. Store any leftovers in an airtight container in the refrigerator for up to 1 week.

2 cups shredded green cabbage

2 cups shredded purple cabbage

1 cup shredded broccoli

½ cup shredded carrots

½ cup shelled edamame

½ cup sliced red bell pepper

¼ cup sliced green onion

¼ cup chopped fresh cilantro

¼ cup chopped cashews, for garnish

1 tsp sesame seeds, for garnish

Crushed red pepper flakes, for garnish (optional)

FOR THE SPICY CASHEW DRESSING

¼ cup cashew butter

¼ cup water

2 tbsp soy sauce

2 tbsp sriracha sauce

1 tsp minced garlic

2 tbsp honey

2 tsp sesame oil

1 tsp rice vinegar

Pinch of salt, or to taste

DINNER

This section offers a variety of unforgettable dinner recipes that will make every meal special. Keep it simple yet satisfying with the **One-Pot Creamy Chicken Mushroom Florentine** (page 186). For quick and delicious options, try the **Korean Ground Beef Rice Bowls** (page 163) or the **Creamy Bacon Carbonara** (page 176). For special occasions, impress your guests with **The Best Lobster Tail** (page 160) or the flavorful **Garlic Butter Herb Prime Rib** (page 158). And don't forget to fire up the grill for the mouthwatering **Grilled Balsamic Honey Soy Flank Steak with Avocado Tomato Salsa** (page 179) or the irresistible **Grilled Hawaiian Pineapple Glazed Shrimp with Rainbow Veggies** (page 193). With these delightful recipes, every dinner will be a delicious and memorable experience.

◀ *Sundays call for a good pot roast, am I right? There is nothing better than a crazy-tender pork roast with potatoes and carrots to bring the family together!*

GARLIC BUTTER HERB PRIME RIB

| SERVES 8 |

This prime rib is melt-in-your-mouth tender, cooked to medium-rare
perfection, and marbled with fat. Seared with a garlic-herb mixture, the meat
soaks up all the flavors, making every single bite insanely delicious.

PREP TIME
5 minutes

COOK TIME
1 hour

TOTAL TIME
1 hour 5 minutes

4–6 lb (2–2.75kg) prime rib, boned
  and tied

1 cup unsalted butter, softened

5 cloves garlic, minced

1 tbsp finely chopped fresh thyme

1 tbsp finely chopped fresh oregano

1 tbsp finely chopped fresh rosemary

1 tbsp salt

1 tsp freshly ground black pepper

1. Remove the prime rib from the refrigerator at least 30 minutes before
   cooking to bring it to room temperature.

2. Preheat the oven to 450°F (230°C).

3. In a small bowl, combine the butter, garlic, thyme, oregano, rosemary,
   salt, and black pepper.

4. Rub the butter mixture all over the outside of the prime rib, and place
   it in a roasting pan or large oven-safe skillet with the fat side up.

5. Cook for 15 minutes. Reduce the oven temperature to 325°F (160°C),
   and bake until the meat reaches an internal temperature of 110°F
   (45°C), about 15 minutes per 1 pound (450g) of meat.

6. Remove the meat from the oven, cover with foil, and let rest for at least
   20 minutes. The temperature will rise to 130°F (55°C) for a medium-rare
   prime rib.

To view on device

THE BEST LOBSTER TAIL

| SERVES 4 |

These decadent lobster tails are smothered with a buttery garlic-herb
sauce and then broiled under high heat. This cooking method makes the lobster
tails tender and juicy. They are a delicious entrée and the ultimate indulgence.

PREP TIME
10 minutes

COOK TIME
10 minutes

TOTAL TIME
20 minutes

4 (6oz/170g) lobster tails

Salt and freshly ground black pepper

¼ cup unsalted butter, melted, plus
   more for serving (optional)

3 cloves garlic, minced

½ tsp sweet paprika

1 tsp minced fresh thyme

1 tsp minced fresh rosemary

1 tsp chopped fresh parsley

To view on device

1. Preheat the broiler to 500°F (260°C).

2. Using kitchen shears, butterfly the lobster tails by cutting down the
   topside center of each. Loosen the meat from the shell, and pull the meat
   upward and out of the shell. Sprinkle the meat with salt and black
   pepper, and place it on a baking sheet.

3. In a small bowl, whisk together the melted butter, garlic, sweet paprika,
   thyme, rosemary, and parsley. Spread evenly on each lobster tail.

4. Broil the lobster tails for about 8 to 10 minutes or until the meat is
   opaque and lightly brown on the top. Serve immediately, with more
   melted butter, if using.

BAKED RIGATONI

| SERVES 6 |

This baked pasta dish offers a delightful combination of flavors that's sure to satisfy everyone at the dinner table. I love using my **Homemade Marinara Sauce** (page 263) for a tangy and delicious tomato base that ties together all the other ingredients.

PREP TIME	COOK TIME	TOTAL TIME
15 minutes	*1 hour 15 minutes*	*1 hour 30 minutes*

1. Preheat the oven to 350°F (175°C). Lightly coat a 9×13-inch (23×33cm) baking pan with cooking spray.

2. In a large pot, cook the rigatoni in boiling water according to the package directions. Drain, return to the pot, and set aside.

3. In a medium saucepan over medium-high heat, add the olive oil, white onion, and garlic, and sauté for 3 minutes or until tender.

4. Add the ground beef and ground sausage. Cook and crumble for 10 minutes or until no longer pink.

5. Add the Easy Italian Seasoning, salt, black pepper, and Homemade Marinara Sauce. Reduce the heat to low, and simmer for 20 minutes.

6. Add the meat sauce to the pasta, and stir until combined.

7. Spread half of the pasta in the bottom of the prepared baking pan. Top with half of the mozzarella cheese and half of the Parmesan cheese. Repeat with the remaining pasta and cheeses.

8. Cover with aluminum foil, and bake for 20 minutes. Remove the foil, and bake for 15 to 20 more minutes or until bubbly. Garnish with basil, and serve hot. Store any leftovers in an airtight container in the refrigerator for up to 4 days.

16oz (450g) uncooked rigatoni pasta

1 tbsp olive oil

1 small white onion, diced

3 cloves garlic, minced

1 lb (450g) lean ground beef

1 lb (450g) ground sausage

1 tbsp **Easy Italian Seasoning** (page 263)

Salt and freshly ground black pepper

1 batch **Homemade Marinara Sauce** (page 263) or 2 (24oz/680g) jars marinara sauce

16oz (450g) shredded mozzarella cheese

½ cup shredded Parmesan cheese

Chopped fresh basil, for garnish

To view on device

SLOW COOKER BEEF BOURGUIGNON

| SERVES 6 |

I love the ease of slow cooker meals, and you can't beat a delicious stew packed with hearty veggies, beef so soft it melts in your mouth, and a rich and flavorful sauce. It's especially nice served with mashed potaotes. Your entire family will love it.

PREP TIME	COOK TIME	TOTAL TIME
20 minutes	*10 hours*	*10 hours 20 minutes*

1. In a large skillet over medium-high heat, cook the bacon for 5 to 7 minutes or until crisp. Transfer the bacon to a 5-quart (4.75-liter) slow cooker.

2. Season the beef chuck with salt and black pepper, add to the skillet, and sear on each side for 2 or 3 minutes. Transfer the beef to the slow cooker.

3. Add the red cooking wine to the skillet, and scrape down the brown bits on the sides of the pan. Simmer the wine for 2 or 3 minutes. Reduce the heat to medium-low, and slowly add the chicken broth, tomato sauce, and soy sauce. Slowly whisk in the all-purpose flour. Add the sauce to the slow cooker.

4. Add the garlic, thyme, carrots, baby tricolor potatoes, and button mushrooms to the slow cooker. Give it a good stir, cover, and cook on low for 8 to 10 hours, or on high for 6 hours, until the beef is tender. Garnish with fresh parsley, and serve.

5 slices bacon, crisp-cooked, drained, and finely chopped

3 lb (1.5kg) boneless beef chuck, cut into 1-in (2.5cm) cubes

Salt and freshly ground black pepper

1 cup red cooking wine

2 cups chicken broth

½ cup tomato sauce

¼ cup soy sauce

¼ cup all-purpose flour

3 cloves garlic, finely chopped

2 tbsp finely chopped fresh thyme

5 medium carrots, peeled and sliced

1 lb (450g) baby tricolor potatoes

8oz (225g) button mushrooms, sliced

Chopped fresh parsley, for garnish

To view on device

KOREAN GROUND BEEF RICE BOWLS

| SERVES 4 |

If my family could pick one meal to eat over and over again, this would be it. These quick and easy rice bowls are a fantastic go-to meal for busy weeknights. They're packed with flavor and will fill you right up.

PREP TIME
5 minutes

COOK TIME
15 minutes

TOTAL TIME
20 minutes

1 lb (450g) lean ground beef

3 cloves garlic, minced

¼ cup packed brown sugar

¼ cup reduced-sodium soy sauce

2 tsp sesame oil

¼ tsp ground ginger

¼ tsp crushed red pepper flakes

¼ tsp freshly ground black pepper

2 cups cooked white or brown rice

2 cups cooked broccoli florets

Sliced green onions, for garnish

Sesame seeds, for garnish

1. In a large skillet over medium heat, cook the ground beef and garlic for 7 to 10 minutes or until no longer pink. Drain and discard the grease.

2. In a small bowl, whisk together the brown sugar, soy sauce, sesame oil, ginger, crushed red pepper flakes, and black pepper. Pour over the ground beef, and let simmer for 1 or 2 minutes.

3. Serve over hot white or brown rice, topped with broccoli florets, and garnished with green onions and sesame seeds.

To view on device

THE BEST SWEDISH MEATBALLS

| SERVES 6 |

These Swedish meatballs are made from scratch, full of flavor, and
smothered with a rich and creamy sauce everyone—even your picky eaters—will like.
Try them served over over egg noodles or rice for a warm, hearty meal.

PREP TIME
15 minutes

COOK TIME
25 minutes

TOTAL TIME
40 minutes

1 lb (450g) ground beef

¼ cup panko breadcrumbs

1 tbsp chopped fresh parsley

¼ tsp ground allspice

¼ tsp ground nutmeg

¼ cup finely chopped white or
    yellow onion

½ tsp garlic powder

½ tsp salt, plus more to taste

⅛ tsp freshly ground black pepper,
    plus more to taste

1 egg

1 tbsp olive oil

5 tbsp unsalted butter

3 tbsp all-purpose flour

2 cups beef broth

1 cup heavy cream

1 tbsp Worcestershire sauce

1 tsp Dijon mustard

1. In a medium bowl, combine the ground beef, panko breadcrumbs, parsley, allspice, nutmeg, white or yellow onion, garlic powder, salt, black pepper, and egg.

2. Portion the beef mixture into 12 large meatballs or 20 small meatballs, and roll into shape.

3. In a large skillet over medium heat, heat the olive oil and 1 tablespoon butter. Add the meatballs in batches, and cook, turning continuously, for 5 to 8 minutes or until brown on every side and cooked through. Transfer to a plate, cover with foil, and repeat with the remaining meatballs.

4. Add the remaining 4 tablespoons butter and the all-purpose flour to the skillet, and whisk for 2 or 3 minutes or until it turns brown. Slowly stir in the beef broth and heavy cream. Add the Worcestershire sauce and Dijon mustard, and bring to a simmer. Cook for 5 minutes or until the sauce starts to thicken. Season with additional salt and black pepper to taste.

5. Add the meatballs to the skillet, simmer for 1 or 2 minutes, and serve.

To view on device

GRILLED CALIFORNIA AVOCADO CHICKEN

| SERVES 4 |

My family loves to cook on the grill, and this juicy chicken is a favorite. It's marinated in a delicious honey garlic balsamic sauce; grilled to perfection; and topped with a thick slice of mozzarella cheese, avocados, tomatoes, and basil. It's a delicious addition to any barbecue.

PREP TIME	COOK TIME	TOTAL TIME
10 minutes + 30 minutes to marinate	*15 minutes*	*55 minutes*

¾ cup balsamic vinegar, plus more for drizzling (optional)

¼ cup honey

3 cloves garlic, minced

2 tbsp olive oil

2 tsp **Easy Italian Seasoning** (page 263)

½ tsp salt, plus more to taste

¼ tsp freshly ground black pepper, plus more to taste

4 boneless, skinless chicken breasts (about 1½ lb/680g)

2 avocados, pitted and diced

3 Roma tomatoes, diced

¼ cup chopped fresh basil

4 slices mozzarella cheese

1. In a medium bowl, whisk together the balsamic vinegar, honey, garlic, olive oil, Easy Italian Seasoning, salt, and black pepper. Add the chicken breasts to the marinade, and turn to coat. Cover with plastic wrap, and place in the refrigerator for 30 minutes to marinate.

2. Meanwhile, in a small bowl, combine the avocados, Roma tomatoes, basil, and salt and pepper to taste.

3. Preheat the grill to medium-high.

4. Remove the chicken from the marinade, and discard the marinade. Grill the chicken for about 6 minutes per side or until cooked throughout and no longer pink.

5. Transfer the chicken to a serving plate, and top each breast with 1 slice mozzarella cheese and some of the avocado, tomato, and basil mixture. Drizzle with more balsamic vinegar, if using, and serve immediately.

To view on device

FRIED AVOCADO TACOS

| SERVES 4 |

Indulge in a crunchy and flavorful delight with these vegetarian tacos. Crispy-fried, yet creamy avocado slices are enveloped in a flavorful coating that kids and adults alike will love. Make them your own by adding your favorite toppings and drizzling with a refreshing cilantro lime dressing.

PREP TIME
15 minutes

COOK TIME
5 minutes

TOTAL TIME
20 minutes

Vegetable oil, for frying

1 cup all-purpose flour

3 eggs

1 cup panko breadcrumbs

1 tbsp **Easy Italian Seasoning** (page 263)

1 tsp garlic powder

1 tsp salt

4 slightly firm avocados, pitted, cut in ½ lengthwise, and sliced

4–6 small flour tortillas

OPTIONAL TOPPINGS

Sliced red onion

Chopped red cabbage

Fresh cilantro

Crumbled cotija cheese

Cilantro lime dressing

1. Add about 1 inch (2.5cm) vegetable oil to a deep skillet, and heat to 350°F (175°C).

2. In a shallow dish, add the all-purpose flour. In another shallow dish, lightly beat the eggs. In a third shallow dish, combine the panko breadcrumbs, Easy Italian Seasoning, garlic powder, and salt.

3. Dip each avocado slice in the flour, then in the egg, and lastly in the panko mixture.

4. Add 4 to 6 battered avocado slices to the hot oil, and fry for about 2 minutes or until golden brown. Using tongs, remove the slices and place on a paper towel–lined plate to drain. Repeat with the remaining slices.

5. Assemble the tacos by laying a flour tortilla on a plate or flat surface. Add a few fried avocado slices and your choice of toppings, drizzle with cilantro lime dressing, if using, and serve.

To view on device

ONE-POT
PAPRIKA ORZO SHRIMP

| SERVES 6 |

This one-pot meal packs a punch, thanks to the paprika. A deliciously creamy
sauce surrounds the shrimp, and the orzo takes it to the next level and really
makes it an entire meal. You'll savor every last bite!

PREP TIME
5 minutes

COOK TIME
20 minutes

TOTAL TIME
25 minutes

2 tbsp unsalted butter

1 cup orzo

2 ½ cups chicken broth

½ cup heavy cream

¼ cup tomato sauce

¼ cup grated Parmesan cheese, plus
more for garnish (optional)

2 tsp sweet paprika

½ tsp salt

¼ tsp freshly ground black pepper

1 lb (450g) large shrimp, peeled and
deveined

¼ cup chopped fresh basil, plus more
for garnish (optional)

1. In a medium skillet over medium-high heat, melt the butter. Add the
   orzo, and cook, stirring often, for 2 or 3 minutes or until slightly golden.

2. Pour in the chicken broth, and bring to a boil. Reduce the heat to
   medium-low, cover, and simmer for 12 to 15 minutes or until the orzo is
   cooked through and fluffed.

3. Add the heavy cream, tomato sauce, Parmesan cheese, paprika, salt,
   black pepper, shrimp, and basil, and stir until incorporated.

4. Cover and simmer for 5 more minutes or until the shrimp turn pink and
   opaque. Garnish with additional Parmesan cheese and basil,
   if using.

SESAME-CRUSTED MISO HONEY SALMON BOWLS

| SERVES 4 |

These salmon bowls not only look beautiful, they also taste amazing! Drizzled with some of my **Spicy Sriracha Mayo** (page 262), these large bowls are hearty and healthy and will fill you right up. I like to peel and roll the carrots to add some visual interest, but you can save time by using shredded carrots instead!

PREP TIME
5 minutes + 30 minutes to marinate

COOK TIME
10 minutes

TOTAL TIME
45 minutes

12oz (340g) salmon fillet (skin on or skinless)

1 tsp kosher salt

½ tsp freshly ground black pepper

½ cup miso paste

4 tbsp soy sauce

4 tbsp honey

2 tbsp rice vinegar

2 tsp sesame oil

4 tbsp white sesame seeds, plus more for garnish

4 tbsp black sesame seeds, plus more for garnish

4 cups cooked white rice

1 avocado, pitted and sliced

1 large carrot, peeled and rolled, or ½ cup shredded carrots

½ cup shredded purple cabbage

½ cup sliced mini cucumbers

½ cup cooked edamame

½ cup **Spicy Sriracha Mayo** (page 262)

Chopped green onions, for garnish

1. Cut the salmon into 1-inch (2.5cm) cubes, and season with kosher salt and black pepper.

2. In a medium bowl, whisk together the miso paste, soy sauce, honey, rice vinegar, sesame oil, and white and black sesame seeds until smooth.

3. Add the salmon to the bowl, and toss to coat. Let marinate at room temperature for 30 minutes.

4. Heat a medium skillet over medium-high heat. Add the salmon in a single layer, and sear on each side for 3 or 4 minutes or until golden brown and cooked to an internal temp of 125°F to 130°F (52°C–54°C). Transfer to a plate.

5. Place 1 cup cooked rice into each of 4 bowls. To each bowl, layer on 3 ounces (85g) cooked salmon, ¼ avocado, 5 or 6 carrot peels (or 2 tablespoons shredded carrots), 2 tablespoons purple cabbage, 2 tablespoons cucumber, and 2 tablespoons edamame.

6. Drizzle 2 tablespoons Spicy Sriracha Mayo on top of each salmon bowl, garnish with green onions and additional sesame seeds, and serve.

20-Minute
BEEF AND BROCCOLI LO MEIN

| SERVES 4 |

As a busy mom of four, I love quick and easy recipes. This lo mein is packed with tender beef flavored with garlic and mixed with noodles and veggies. The sauce is incredibly delicious, which makes this a regular meal in our house— not to mention it only takes 20 minutes from start to finish!

PREP TIME	COOK TIME	TOTAL TIME
5 minutes	*15 minutes*	*20 minutes*

8oz (225g) uncooked lo mein noodles or spaghetti noodles

3 cups fresh broccoli florets

1 tbsp olive oil

8oz (225g) flank steak, sliced against the grain into ¼-in (0.5cm) strips

3 cloves garlic, minced

1 medium carrot, shredded

¼ cup packed brown sugar

¼ cup reduced-sodium soy sauce

2 tbsp hoisin sauce

2 tsp sesame oil

¼ tsp ground ginger

¼ tsp crushed red pepper flakes

¼ tsp freshly ground black pepper

Chopped green onions, for garnish

Sesame seeds, for garnish

1. In a large pot, cook the lo mein noodles in boiling water according to the package directions.

2. Add the broccoli during the last 5 minutes of the noodle cook time, and cook until tender. Drain the noodles and broccoli.

3. While the noodles and broccoli are cooking, heat the olive oil in a medium skillet over medium-high heat. Add the flank steak, and cook for 2 or 3 minutes per side or until no longer pink.

4. Reduce the heat to low. Add the garlic and carrot, and cook for 1 minute.

5. In a small bowl, whisk together the brown sugar, soy sauce, hoisin sauce, sesame oil, ginger, crushed red pepper flakes, and black pepper.

6. Add the cooked noodles to the skillet, pour the sauce on top, and toss until incorporated. Garnish with green onions and sesame seeds, and serve.

To view on device

THE BEST HOMEMADE CHILI

| SERVES 8 |

Thick, rich, and flavorful, this chili will become a must-make recipe in your home. It's full of lean ground beef, two kinds of beans, ripe tomatoes, and fresh seasonings. Make it your own with your favorite toppings, such as shredded cheddar cheese and sliced green onions, and you won't be able to resist seconds. It's great with fresh cornbread.

PREP TIME	COOK TIME	TOTAL TIME
15 minutes	*45 minutes*	*60 minutes*

1. In a large pot over medium-high heat, heat the olive oil. Add the onion, green bell pepper, and garlic, and sauté for 2 or 3 minutes or until almost tender.

2. Add the ground beef, and cook, crumbling, for 4 or 5 minutes or until brown.

3. Add the beef broth, tomato sauce, diced tomatoes, pinto beans, kidney beans, chili powder, oregano, cumin, coriander, salt, and cayenne to the pot.

4. Bring to a boil, reduce the heat to medium-low, and simmer for about 30 minutes or until the chili thickens and the flavors combine.

5. Garnish with your choice of toppings, and serve. Store any leftovers in an airtight container in the refrigerator for up to 4 days.

1 tbsp olive oil

1 small white onion, diced

1 green bell pepper, ribs and seeds removed, and diced

2 cloves garlic, minced

2 lb (1kg) lean ground beef

2 cups beef broth

1 (8oz/225g) can tomato sauce

1 (15oz/425g) can diced tomatoes

1 (15oz/425g) can pinto beans, drained and rinsed

1 (15oz/425g) can red kidney beans, drained and rinsed

3 tbsp chili powder

1 tbsp dried oregano

1 tsp ground cumin

1 tsp ground coriander

1 tsp salt

¼ tsp cayenne

To view on device

MELT-IN-YOUR-MOUTH POT ROAST

| SERVES 6 |

This pot roast is our go-to for family dinners. The meat is deliciously tender, and it's slow cooked with delicate potatoes, flavorful onions, and sweet carrots in a perfectly seasoned broth. The recipe is super simple, and you definitely won't be able to resist coming back for seconds.

PREP TIME	COOK TIME	TOTAL TIME
10 minutes	*70 minutes–10 hours*	*80 minutes–10 hours 10 minutes*

2 cups beef broth

½ cup red wine

3 tbsp Worcestershire sauce

3 cloves garlic, minced

1 tsp onion powder

1 tsp garlic powder

1 tsp salt, plus more for seasoning

½ tsp freshly ground black pepper, plus more for seasoning

3–4 lb (1.5–2kg) chuck roast

2 tbsp olive oil

4 large carrots, sliced

1 lb (450g) baby potatoes, skin on

1 yellow onion, chopped into large pieces

Sprigs fresh rosemary, for garnish

Chopped fresh parsley, for garnish

1. In a small bowl, combine the beef broth, red wine, Worcestershire sauce, garlic, onion powder, garlic powder, salt, and black pepper. Set aside.

2. Sprinkle more salt and black pepper on each side of the chuck roast. Cut the roast if necessary to fit in your choice of cookware. Set aside.

To cook in a slow cooker

1. In a large cast-iron skillet over medium-high heat, heat the olive oil until it starts smoking. Add the seasoned roast, and sear for 2 or 3 minutes per side for a dark brown crust.

2. In a 5-quart (4.75-liter) slow cooker, add the carrots, baby potatoes, and yellow onion. Place the roast on top, and pour the broth mixture over all. Cover and cook on low for 10 hours or until tender. Garnish with rosemary and parsley, and serve.

To cook in an Instant Pot

1. Press the sauté button on the Instant Pot and wait for it to read HOT before adding the olive oil. Working in batches if necessary, sear the seasoned roast in the Instant Pot for 2 or 3 minutes per side. Transfer the seared roast to a plate.

2. Place the carrots, baby potatoes, and yellow onion in the bottom of the Instant Pot. Add the roast on top, and pour the broth mixture over all. Cover and cook on high pressure for 60 minutes and then do a natural release. Garnish with rosemary and parsley, and serve.

To roast in the oven

1. Preheat the oven to 425°F (220°C).

2. In a large cast-iron skillet over medium-high heat, heat the olive oil until it starts smoking. Add the seasoned roast, and sear for 2 or 3 minutes per side for a dark brown crust.

To view on device

3. In a large casserole dish, add the carrots, baby potatoes, and yellow onion. Place the roast on top, and pour the broth mixture over all. Cover tightly and roast for 30 minutes. Turn the oven down to 300°F (150°C), and continue cooking for 4 or 5 hours. Garnish with rosemary and parsley, and serve.

CREAMY BACON CARBONARA

| SERVES 6 |

This classic pasta dish features a creamy, savory sauce; crispy bacon; and sautéed onions and mushrooms that combine for the perfect balance of smoky, sweet, and earthy flavors. Every bite is a delightful blend of richness and indulgence.

PREP TIME	COOK TIME	TOTAL TIME
15 minutes	*15 minutes*	*30 minutes*

1. In a large pot, cook the spaghetti in boiling water according to the package directions.

2. Meanwhile, in a medium bowl, beat together the eggs, cream, Parmesan cheese, parsley, salt, and crushed red pepper flakes. Set aside.

3. In a large skillet over medium-high heat, fry the bacon for 5 or 6 minutes or until crisp. Transfer the bacon to a paper towel–lined plate to drain, crumble, and set aside. Reserve 1 or 2 tablespoons of the bacon grease in the skillet.

4. Add the button mushrooms and white onion to the skillet, and sauté in the reserved bacon grease for 5 minutes or until the onions are translucent and golden and the mushrooms are brown.

5. Drain the pasta, and while it's still warm, add it to the skillet.

6. Pour the cream mixture over the pasta, and stir over low heat for 1 or 2 minutes. Be sure you do this over *low* heat, or you will make scrambled eggs.

7. Remove from the heat, stir in the crumbled bacon, garnish with parsley and Parmesan, and serve.

8oz (225g) spaghetti or your choice of pasta

2 eggs

¼ cup cream or heavy cream

⅓ cup grated Parmesan cheese, plus more for garnish

1 tsp chopped fresh parsley, plus more for garnish

¼ tsp salt

½ tsp crushed red pepper flakes

½ lb (225g) bacon

3 button mushrooms, chopped

1 small white onion, chopped

To view on device

SLOW COOKER MISSISSIPPI PORK ROAST

| SERVES 6 |

This savory pot roast is slow cooked all day to yield a tender and juicy meat that goes perfectly with mashed potatoes and some warm, fluffy rolls. Every bite of the sweet and spicy pork will melt in your mouth.

PREP TIME	COOK TIME	TOTAL TIME
5 minutes	*6 hours*	*6 hours 5 minutes*

1. Add the pork roast to a 5-quart (4.75-liter) slow cooker.

2. Sprinkle the ranch seasoning mix and the au jus gravy mix over the roast. Top with the butter and pepperoncini.

3. Cover, and cook on low for 6 hours.

4. Shred with a fork, and serve.

2 lb (1kg) marinated fresh pork roast

1 (1oz/30g) package ranch seasoning mix (2 tbsp)

1 (1oz/30g) packet au jus gravy mix (2 tbsp)

½ stick (4 tbsp) unsalted butter, sliced

8–10 pepperoncini (banana peppers)

To view on device

GRILLED BALSAMIC HONEY SOY FLANK STEAK
with Avocado Tomato Salsa

| SERVES 6 |

Tender flank steak is marinated in a delicious blend of balsamic vinegar, honey, soy sauce, garlic, and herbs; grilled to perfection; and topped with a refreshing avocado tomato salsa. A drizzle of balsamic glaze adds a finishing touch to this mouthwatering dish.

PREP TIME
10 minutes + 1 hour to marinate

COOK TIME
12 minutes

TOTAL TIME
1 hour 22 minutes

2 lb (1kg) flank steak

Balsamic glaze, for garnish

FOR THE BALSAMIC HONEY SOY MARINADE

¼ cup balsamic vinegar

¼ cup honey

2 tbsp soy sauce

3 cloves garlic, minced

1 tbsp minced white onion

2 tbsp olive oil

1 tbsp **Easy Italian Seasoning** (page 263)

Juice of 1 lime

FOR THE AVOCADO TOMATO SALSA

2 avocados, pitted and diced

2 Roma tomatoes, diced

¼ red onion, diced

1 jalapeño, diced

¼ cup chopped fresh cilantro

Juice of 1 lime

Salt and freshly ground black pepper

1. To make the balsamic honey soy marinade, in a large bowl or zipper-lock bag, combine the balsamic vinegar, honey, soy sauce, garlic, white onion, olive oil, Easy Italian Seasoning, and lime juice.

2. Add the flank steak to the marinade, cover the bowl with plastic wrap or seal the bag, and place in the refrigerate for 1 hour or overnight to marinate.

3. Preheat the grill to high heat. Remove the steak from the marinade, discard the marinade, and add the steak to the grill. Sear the steak over high heat for 1 or 2 minutes per side and then move the steak to indirect heat and cook until your desired doneness. (Medium-rare is 135°F/60°C.) Remove the steak from the grill, cover with foil, and set aside to rest for 10 minutes.

4. In a medium bowl, combine the avocados, Roma tomatoes, red onion, jalapeño, cilantro, and lime juice. Season with salt and black pepper.

5. Slice the steak across the grain, and top with the avocado tomato salsa. Drizzle with a little balsamic glaze, and serve.

PERFECTLY TENDER LONDON BROIL

| SERVES 6 |

This decadent London broil is the perfect main course and will impress
even the pickiest of guests. I love cooking this recipe because it is quick and easy,
yet the finished dish looks like I spent all day in the kitchen making it. The meat marinates
from 2 hours to overnight, which makes it perfectly tender and packed with flavor.

PREP TIME
10 minutes + 2 hours to marinate

COOK TIME
20 minutes

TOTAL TIME
2 hours 30 minutes

⅓ cup soy sauce

⅓ cup freshly squeezed lemon juice

½ cup olive oil

¼ cup Worchestershire sauce

1 tbsp minced garlic

2 tbsp **Easy Italian Seasoning** (page 263)

½ tsp salt

1 tsp freshly ground black pepper

Pinch of crushed red pepper flakes

2 lb (1kg) London broil round steak

1. Prepare the marinade by adding the soy sauce, lemon juice, olive oil, Worcestershire sauce, garlic, Easy Italian Seasoning, salt, black pepper, and crushed red pepper flakes to a 1-gallon (3.75-liter) zipper-lock bag. Add the London broil round steak, seal the bag, and marinate in the refrigerator for at least 2 hours or overnight.

2. Preheat the broiler to high heat.

3. Transfer the steak from the marinade into a 9×13-inch (23×33cm) baking dish, and discard any remaining marinade. Broil for 5 or 6 minutes on the center rack and then flip to the other side and broil for 3 or 4 more minutes or until it reaches an internal temperature of 135°F (58°C) for medium rare or 145°F (63°C) for medium well.

4. Let the steak rest for 10 minutes before slicing it against the grain. This will make the meat tender and juicy.

NOTE

I know it's tempting to slice the meat right out of the oven, but trust me when I say you *must* let it rest for at least 10 minutes before doing so. Letting meat rest allows it to absorb all the juices and makes it so tender.

To view on device

CHICKEN ALFREDO ROLL-UPS

| SERVES 8 |

These roll-ups are easily one of my family's favorite meals. Made with my homemade
Family Favorite Alfredo Sauce (page 202), these chicken roll-ups are perfect for even
the pickiest of eaters. They're the perfect quick and easy dish everyone will love.

PREP TIME
10 minutes

COOK TIME
40 minutes

TOTAL TIME
50 minutes

8 lasagna noodles

1 batch **Family Favorite Alfredo Sauce**
(page 202)

2 cups cooked and shredded chicken
(I use a rotisserie chicken.)

2 cups shredded mozzarella cheese

NOTE

I like to add bacon to these roll-ups.
Cook 1 pound (450g) bacon, crumble
it, and add it with the chicken. It's extra
delicious!

To view on device

1. Preheat oven to 350°F (175°C). Lightly coat a 9×13-inch (23×33cm) baking pan with cooking spray.

2. In a large pot, cook the lasagna noodles in boiling water according to the package directions until al dente. Drain and rinse in cold water, and lay the noodles on a paper towel to remove excess water.

3. Evenly spread 1 cup Family Favorite Alfredo Sauce in the bottom of the prepared baking pan.

4. Place the noodles in the pan. Spread 2 tablespoons Alfredo sauce over each lasagna noodle. Add 2 tablespoons shredded chicken evenly over each noodle, and top with about 3 tablespoons mozzarella cheese. Carefully roll up each lasagna noodle, and place them seam side down in the baking pan. Repeat with the remaining noodles.

5. Pour the remaining Alfredo sauce over all the roll-ups, and top with the remaining mozzarella.

6. Bake for about 30 minutes or until heated through and the cheese is bubbly.

GARLIC BUTTER AND HERB STEAK BITES WITH POTATOES

| SERVES 5 |

These delicious steak bites are seared to perfection in a cast-iron skillet alongside seasoned potatoes and finished with a sprinkle of fresh herbs for a delightful burst of freshness. My family loves this recipe and eats every last bite.

PREP TIME
5 minutes

COOK TIME
20 minutes

TOTAL TIME
25 minutes

1 tbsp olive oil

2 tbsp unsalted butter

1 lb (450g) Yukon Gold potatoes, cut in ½-in (1.25cm) pieces

3 cloves garlic, minced

1 tsp chopped fresh thyme, plus more for garnish

1 tsp chopped fresh rosemary, plus more for garnish

1 tsp chopped fresh oregano, plus more for garnish

1¼ lb (565g) sirloin steak, cut into 1-in (2.5cm) cubes

Salt and freshly ground black pepper

1. In a large cast-iron skillet over medium-high heat, heat the olive oil and 1 tablespoon butter. Add the Yukon Gold potatoes, garlic, thyme, rosemary, and oregano, and cook for about 3 minutes. Stir and cook for 3 more minutes or until the potatoes are fork-tender. Transfer the potatoes to a plate, and set aside.

2. Increase the heat to high, and sprinkle the salt and paper on the steak. Add the sirloin steak and the remaining 1 tablespoon butter to the skillet. Let the steak sear for 1 minute and then cook, stirring continually, for 4 or 5 minutes or until golden brown.

3. Transfer to a serving dish, top with more chopped fresh herbs, and serve.

To view on device

CREAMY CHICKEN MARSALA

| SERVES 4 |

Perfectly moist chicken is smothered in a creamy sauce that's packed full of flavor. This classic Italian dish tastes like it came from a restaurant and is a favorite at our house. Ready in under 30 minutes, this easy dinner recipe will be one of the best things you make!

PREP TIME
5 minutes

COOK TIME
20 minutes

TOTAL TIME
25 minutes

2 tbsp olive oil

4 boneless, skinless chicken breasts (about 1½ lb/680g)

Salt and freshly ground black pepper

1½ cups sliced button mushrooms

½ cup Marsala wine

½ cup chicken broth

1 cup heavy whipping cream

1 tsp dry ground mustard

1 tsp garlic powder

Chopped fresh parsley, for garnish

1. In a large skillet over medium heat, heat 1 tablespoon olive oil. Add the chicken, lightly season with salt and black pepper, and cook for 3 or 4 minutes per side or until the chicken is lightly browned and cooked through. Transfer the chicken to a plate, and set aside.

2. Add the remaining 1 tablespoon olive oil to the skillet, and sauté the mushrooms for 1 or 2 minutes.

3. Add the Marsala wine. Increase the heat to medium-high, bring to a boil, and cook for 1 or 2 minutes to burn off the alcohol.

4. Add the chicken broth, heavy whipping cream, dry mustard, and garlic powder, and bring to a boil. Reduce the heat to medium-low, and simmer for about 10 minutes or until the sauce starts to thicken.

5. Return the cooked chicken to the skillet, and simmer for 1 or 2 more minutes. Garnish with fresh parsley, and serve.

NOTE

The alcohol will burn out during the cooking process, but if you are worried about cooking with wine, you can substitute ¼ cup white grape juice, 1 tablespoon vanilla extract, and 2 tablespoons sherry vinegar.

To view on device

One-Pot
CREAMY CHICKEN MUSHROOM FLORENTINE

| SERVES 4 |

We are constantly on the go at my house, so quick and easy meals are a must. This hearty meal is simple to prepare and can be made in one pan in just 30 minutes. Filled with sun-dried tomatoes, spinach, mushrooms, and the creamiest pasta, this recipe checks all the comfort-food boxes.

PREP TIME	COOK TIME	TOTAL TIME
10 minutes	*20 minutes*	*30 minutes*

1 tbsp unsalted butter

1 lb (450g) boneless, skinless chicken breasts, cut into 1-in (2.5cm) pieces

1 tsp olive oil

2 cloves garlic, minced

¼ cup sun-dried tomatoes, drained

4oz (115g) button mushrooms, sliced

1 tbsp all-purpose flour

2 cups chicken broth

1½ cups half-and-half

1 tsp salt

¼ tsp freshly ground black pepper

½ tsp garlic powder

8oz (225g) linguine, broken in half

¼ cup grated Parmesan cheese

2 cups baby spinach

1. In a large skillet over medium-high heat, heat the butter. Add the chicken, and cook for 3 or 4 minutes or until golden brown and no longer pink.

2. Add the olive oil, garlic, sun-dried tomatoes, and mushrooms, and cook for 4 or 5 minutes or until tender.

3. Add the all-purpose flour, and cook for 1 more minute.

4. Slowly whisk in the chicken broth, half-and-half, salt, black pepper, and garlic powder until incorporated.

5. Add the linguine. Bring to a simmer, cover, and cook for 10 to 15 minutes or until the pasta is tender.

6. Remove from the heat, add the Parmesan cheese and baby spinach, and stir until the spinach starts to wilt. Serve immediately.

To view on device

AMAZING STREET TACOS

| SERVES 6 |

Satisfy your taco cravings with this mouthwatering street taco recipe. Bite-size flank steak is marinated in a flavorful sauce, cooked to juicy perfection, tucked into tortillas, and loaded with your favorite toppings. It's a flavor-packed fiesta you won't want to miss!

PREP TIME	COOK TIME	TOTAL TIME
10 minutes + 1–2 hours to marinate	*7 minutes*	*2 hours 17 minutes*

1. In a medium bowl, combine the soy sauce, Worcestershire sauce, lime juice, garlic, cilantro, chili powder, cumin, salt, and black pepper.

2. Add the flank steak, cover the bowl with plastic wrap, and place in the refrigerator to marinate for 1 or 2 hours.

3. Heat a medium skillet over medium-high heat. Add the steak and marinade, and cook for 5 to 7 minutes or until the steak is no longer pink.

4. Evenly divide the steak among the tortillas, top with your desired toppings, and serve.

½ cup soy sauce

1 tbsp Worcestershire sauce

Juice of 1 lime

3 cloves garlic, minced

2 tbsp chopped fresh cilantro

1 tsp chili powder

½ tsp ground cumin

Salt and freshly ground black pepper

1 lb (450g) flank steak or skirt steak, cut into 1-in (2.5cm) pieces

6–8 small flour or corn tortillas

OPTIONAL TOPPINGS

Chopped Roma tomatoes

Chopped red onion

Diced avocado

Chopped fresh cilantro

Grated cotija cheese

To view on device

BAKED SWEET AND SOUR CHICKEN

| SERVES 6 |

This might be my all-time favorite recipe to make for my family. The chicken is
crispy on the outside, tender and juicy on the inside, and packed with so much flavor.
It pairs perfectly with my **Easy Fried Rice** (page 141).

PREP TIME
20 minutes

COOK TIME
1 hour

TOTAL TIME
1 hour 20 minutes

4 boneless, skinless chicken breasts
   (about 1½ lb/680g)

Salt and freshly ground black pepper

1½ cups cornstarch

3 eggs, lightly beaten

¼ cup canola oil

1 cup granulated sugar

¼ cup ketchup

¼ cup apple cider vinegar

¼ cup white vinegar

1 tbsp reduced-sodium soy sauce

1 tsp garlic salt

Chopped green onions, for garnish

Sesame seeds, for garnish

1. Preheat the oven to 325°F (165°C). Spray a 9×13-inch (23×33cm) baking dish with cooking spray.

2. Cut the chicken breasts into bite-size pieces, and season them with salt and black pepper.

3. In separate medium bowls, place the cornstarch and eggs. Dip the chicken pieces in the cornstarch and then coat in the eggs.

4. In a large skillet over medium-high heat, heat the canola oil. Add the chicken, and cook for 2 or 3 minutes or until browned. Transfer the chicken to the prepared baking dish.

5. In a medium bowl, combine the sugar, ketchup, apple cider vinegar, white vinegar, soy sauce, and garlic salt. Pour over the chicken.

6. Bake for 1 hour, stirring the chicken every 15 minutes to ensure it's coated in the sauce. Garnish with green onions and sesame seeds, and serve.

To view on device

CHICKEN ENCHILADAS
with Avocado Cream Sauce

| SERVES 6 |

*I love enchiladas, but wait until you try this chicken and veggie version
with its creamy avocado sauce! The sauce is baked into the enchiladas and drizzled
on top so you get a double dose of that creamy, delicious avocado-filled taste.*

PREP TIME
20 minutes

COOK TIME
20 minutes

TOTAL TIME
40 minutes

FOR THE SAUCE

2 tbsp unsalted butter

2 tbsp all-purpose flour

2 cups chicken broth

¾ cup sour cream, plus more for
garnish (optional)

½ tsp ground cumin

½ tsp salt

½ tsp garlic powder

¼ tsp freshly ground black pepper

2 avocados, pitted

½ cup chopped fresh cilantro, plus
more for garnish (optional)

Juice of 1 lime

FOR THE ENCHILADAS

2 tbsp olive oil

1 medium white or yellow onion,
peeled and thinly sliced

2 poblano peppers, stemmed and
thinly sliced

1 jalapeño, finely diced

8–10 flour tortillas

4 cups cooked and shredded chicken
(I use a rotisserie chicken.)

2–3 cups shredded Monterey Jack
cheese, plus more for garnish
(optional)

1. Preheat the oven to 350°F (175°C).

2. To make the avocado cream sauce, melt the butter in a large skillet over medium-high heat. Add the flour, and cook, whisking, for 2 or 3 minutes or until golden and bubbly. Slowly whisk in the chicken broth. Bring to a boil, reduce the heat to medium-low, and simmer for 5 minutes.

3. Stir in the sour cream, cumin, salt, garlic powder, and black pepper, whisking if necessary to remove any lumps. Transfer the mixture to a blender or food processor. Add the avocados, cilantro, and lime juice, and pulse until smooth and well blended. (Be very careful blending hot liquids. The heat will expand, so be sure to remove the lid occasionally to allow the heat to escape.) Season with additional salt or pepper if needed.

4. In a large skillet over medium-high heat, heat the olive oil. Add the onion, poblanos, and jalapeño, and sauté for 5 or 6 minutes or until the onions are cooked and translucent. Remove from the heat.

5. To assemble the enchiladas, place a tortilla on a flat surface. Spread 1 or 2 tablespoons avocado cream sauce down the middle of the tortilla. Layer on some of the vegetable mixture, shredded chicken, and Monterey Jack cheese. Carefully roll the tortilla, and place it seam side down in the baking dish. Repeat with the remaining tortillas. Drizzle the top with about half of the remaining avocado cream sauce, cover the dish with foil, and bake for 20 minutes or until the tortillas are heated.

6. Remove from the oven, and drizzle the remaining avocado cream sauce over the top. Garnish with additional cilantro, sour cream, and cheese, if using, and serve.

To view on device

LEMON GARLIC SHRIMP PASTA

| SERVES 6 |

This elegant pasta dish will impress any guest, but perhaps even better, it's so quick and easy to make and is prepared in one pot, which makes cleanup a breeze. Fresh shrimp is cooked in a buttery lemon garlic sauce and then tossed with Parmesan cheese and pasta—delicious!

PREP TIME	COOK TIME	TOTAL TIME
5 minutes	20 minutes	25 minutes

8oz (225g) uncooked linguine

2 tbsp olive oil

6 tbsp unsalted butter

4 cloves garlic, minced

1 tsp crushed red pepper flakes

1¼ lb (565g) large shrimp, peeled and deveined

Salt and freshly ground black pepper

1 tsp **Easy Italian Seasoning** (page 263)

4 cups baby spinach

¾ cup shredded Parmesan cheese

2 tbsp chopped fresh parsley

1 tbsp freshly squeezed lemon juice

1. In a large pot, cook the linguine in boiling water according to the package directions. Drain and set aside.

2. Using the same pot, heat the olive oil and 2 tablespoons butter. Add the garlic and crushed red pepper flakes, and cook for 1 or 2 minutes or until fragrant.

3. Add the shrimp and salt and black pepper to taste. Cook for 4 or 5 minutes or until the shrimp start to turn pink.

4. Add the Easy Italian Seasoning and baby spinach, and cook for 2 or 3 minutes or until the spinach is wilted.

5. Return the linguine to the pot with the remaining 4 tablespoons butter, ½ cup Parmesan cheese, and the parsley. Stir until mixed and the butter is melted.

6. Add the lemon juice, toss, sprinkle remaining ¼ cup Parmesan cheese over the top, and serve immediately.

To view on device

GRILLED HAWAIIAN PINEAPPLE GLAZED SHRIMP
with Rainbow Veggies

| SERVES 6 |

These sweet and tangy shrimp and veggie skewers are coated in a mouthwatering brown sugar and soy sauce marinade. They are caramelized to perfection, creating a burst of flavor in every bite.

PREP TIME
10 minutes + 30 minutes to marinate

COOK TIME
10 minutes

TOTAL TIME
50 minutes

1. In a small saucepan, whisk together the brown sugar, soy sauce, pineapple juice, garlic, salt, and black pepper.

2. In a small bowl, whisk together the water and cornstarch. Slowly whisk the cornstarch mixture into the brown sugar mixture.

3. Set the saucepan over medium-high heat, bring to a boil, and boil for 1 to 3 minutes or until the mixture thickens. Remove from the heat. Reserve ¼ cup of the sauce for later use.

4. Add the shrimp to the saucepan with the remaining sauce, and set in the refrigerator to marinate for at least 30 minutes.

5. Preheat the grill to medium-high heat.

6. Remove the shrimp from the marinade, discard the marinade, and thread the shrimp on skewers, alternating with the red bell pepper, yellow bell pepper, zucchini, red onion, and pineapple pieces.

7. Grill the skewers for about 3 minutes per side or until cooked through. Drizzle with the reserved sauce, garnish with cilantro, and serve.

½ cup packed brown sugar

½ cup soy sauce

¼ cup pineapple juice

2 cloves garlic, minced

½ tsp salt

¼ tsp freshly ground black pepper

1 tbsp water

1 tbsp cornstarch

1 lb (450g) large shrimp, peeled and deveined

1 red bell pepper, ribs and seeds removed, and cut into 1-in (2.5cm) cubes

1 yellow bell pepper, ribs and seeds removed, and cut into 1-in (2.5cm) cubes

1 zucchini, sliced into rounds

1 red onion, cut into 1-in (2.5cm) pieces

2 cups fresh pineapple, cut into 1-in (2.5cm) cubes

Fresh cilantro, for garnish

HOMEMADE PIEROGI

| SERVES 8 |

These delicious Polish dumplings are made with a savory dough and filled with a mixture of mashed potatoes, cheese, and onions. Each pierogi is carefully made, with the dough tightly pinched closed to ensure the filling remains intact during cooking, resulting in a comforting and satisfying dish.

PREP TIME
20 minutes + 30 minutes to rest

COOK TIME
45 minutes

TOTAL TIME
1 hour 35 minutes

4 cups all-purpose flour

3 tsp salt

½ cup vegetable oil

2 large eggs

¾ cup warm water

2 medium russet potatoes, peeled and chopped large

5 tbsp unsalted butter

¼ cup cottage cheese or sour cream

1 cup shredded cheddar cheese

1 small sweet onion, chopped

Sliced green onions, for garnish

1. In a large bowl, and using a mixer fitted with a dough hook on low, combine the all-purpose flour, 2 teaspoons salt, vegetable oil, eggs, and warm water. Increase the speed to medium-high, and mix for 5 or 6 minutes or until the dough is smooth and springy. Transfer the dough to another large, oiled bowl, and turn the dough a few times so it is evenly coated with the oil. Cover the bowl with a towel, and let the dough rest for 30 minutes.

2. Meanwhile, add the russet potatoes to a large pot. Add enough water to cover the potatoes by 1 inch (2.5cm), set over high heat, and bring to a boil. Boil for 20 to 25 minutes or until the potatoes are fork-tender. Drain, and allow to cool for 5 to 10 minutes.

3. Mash the potatoes well. Add 2 tablespoons butter, cottage cheese, cheddar cheese, and remaining 1 teaspoon salt, and stir to combine.

4. Cut the rested dough into two equal pieces. Cover one piece with plastic wrap to prevent it from drying out, and set aside. Roll out the other piece on a floured surface until it is ⅛ inch (3mm) thick. Using a 3-inch (7.5cm) round cookie cutter, cut out dough circles as close together as possible to maximize the amount of usable dough.

5. Add about ½ tablespoon of the potato mixture to the center of each dough circle, fold the dough over the filling, and tightly pinch the edges together to seal in the filling. Be sure to really pinch the dough together because you don't want the filling to escape. Repeat with the remaining dough and filling.

6. In a large skillet over medium-low heat, cook the sweet onion in the remaining 3 tablespoons butter for about 12 minutes or until the onions are browned.

7. Bring a large pot of salted water to a boil over high heat. Working in two batches, boil the pierogi for about 3 minutes or until they float. Using a slotted spoon, transfer the pierogi to the skillet with the cooked onions. Cook over medium heat for 2 or 3 minutes, garnish with green onions, and serve hot.

To view on device

GARLIC AND HERB–CRUSTED PORK TENDERLOIN

| SERVES 8 |

Elevate your pork tenderloin game with this easy and flavorful recipe. Slathered in stone-ground mustard and a blend of herbs and spices, this roasted tenderloin is a guaranteed hit.

PREP TIME
5 minutes

COOK TIME
1 hour 15 minutes

TOTAL TIME
1 hour 20 minutes

3–4 lb (1.5–2kg) pork tenderloin

2 tbsp stone-ground mustard

2 tbsp olive oil

6 cloves garlic, minced

2 tbsp dried basil

2 tbsp dried thyme

2 tbsp dried rosemary

2 tsp ground sage

2 tsp salt

1 tsp freshly ground coarse black pepper

1. Preheat the oven to 400°F (205°C).

2. Place the pork tenderloin on a baking sheet. Spread the stone-ground mustard evenly on both sides of the pork.

3. In a small bowl, combine the olive oil, garlic, basil, thyme, rosemary, sage, salt, and black pepper. Spread the herb mixture evenly over the top and sides of the pork.

4. Roast for 1 hour 15 minutes or until the pork reaches an internal temperature of 155°F (70°C).

5. Remove from the oven, and let rest for 10 minutes before slicing and serving.

NOTE

The rule of thumb for cooking a pork tenderloin is about 25 minutes per 1 pound (450g).

SLOW COOKER GENERAL TSO'S CHICKEN

| SERVES 5 |

I love slow cooker meals because they take very little time and preparation yet are some of the most flavorful dishes. This General Tso's Chicken is coated in an amazingly sweet and savory sauce that has a small kick of heat. Trust me when I tell you it's better than any take-out version you can find.

PREP TIME	COOK TIME	TOTAL TIME
5 minutes	*4 hours*	*4 hours 5 minutes*

4 boneless, skinless chicken breasts (about 1½ lb/680g), cut into 1-in (2.5cm) cubes

¼ cup cornstarch

1 tbsp vegetable oil

½ cup hoisin sauce

2 tbsp soy sauce

½ cup packed brown sugar

3 cloves garlic, minced

3 tbsp rice wine vinegar

1 tsp sesame oil

¼ tsp ground ginger

½ tsp crushed red pepper flakes, or to taste, plus more for garnish (optional)

2 cups cooked white rice

Sliced green onions, for garnish

Sesame seeds, for garnish

1. In a large bowl, add the chicken and cornstarch, and toss until the chicken is completely coated in the cornstarch.

2. In a medium skillet over medium-high heat, heat the vegetable oil. Add the coated chicken, and cook for 3 or 4 minutes or until lightly brown but not cooked through. Transfer the chicken to a 5-quart (4.75-liter) slow cooker.

3. In a small bowl, whisk together the hoisin sauce, soy sauce, brown sugar, garlic, rice wine vinegar, sesame oil, ginger, and crushed red pepper flakes. Pour over the chicken in the slow cooker.

4. Cover and cook on low heat for 3 or 4 hours or until the chicken is cooked through.

5. Serve over cooked rice, garnished with green onions, sesame seeds, and additional crushed red pepper flakes, if using.

NOTE

For a thicker sauce, remove the cooked chicken from the slow cooker, add 1 tablespoon cornstarch to the sauce, and mix well. Return the chicken to the slow cooker, and cook for 15 more minutes or until the sauce thickens.

To view on device

NEW YORK STEAK

| SERVES 2 |

My son loves steak. He always wants to cook it and is constantly trying new recipes and gadgets to help him achieve the perfect steak. He developed this recipe, and I must say, it's the best of the best. This skillet-seared New York Steak is tender, juicy, and full of flavor.

PREP TIME
5 minutes

COOK TIME
15 minutes

TOTAL TIME
20 minutes

2 (8oz–10oz/225g–285g) New York strip steaks

Salt and freshly ground black pepper

2 tbsp olive oil

½ cup unsalted butter

8 cloves garlic, smashed

Sprigs of fresh rosemary and thyme

1. Let the New York strip steaks rest for 30 minutes to come to room temperature and then season with salt and black pepper.

2. In a medium skillet over medium-high heat, heat the olive oil. When it starts to smoke, add the steaks to the skillet, and sear for 3 or 4 minutes per side until the steak has a golden brown crust.

3. Add the butter and let it melt in the skillet.

4. Add the garlic, rosemary, and thyme.

5. Reduce the heat to medium, and cook, occasionally spooning the butter over the steaks, for 2 or 3 minutes or until they reach the desired internal temperature (see Note).

NOTE

How do you like your steak? Here are the internal temperatures of steak for rare through well-done:
- Rare: 130°F (55°C)
- Medium-rare: 135°F (58°C)
- Medium: 145°F (63°C)
- Medium-well: 155°F (69°C)
- Well: Over 160°F (71°C)

You can finish the steaks in the oven instead of on the stove. After you sear each side, put the steaks in a cast-iron skillet; add the butter, garlic, rosemary, and thyme; and cook in a 425°F (220°C) oven until they reach the desired internal temperature.

To view on device

DELICIOUS GARLICKY SHRIMP SCAMPI

| SERVES 4 |

If you are looking for a delicious shrimp entrée, this is it. This recipe takes less than 15 minutes from start to finish and tastes amazing served over warm pasta. I like to finish off my scampi with a Parmesan-breadcrumb topping, which really sets it apart.

PREP TIME
5 minutes

COOK TIME
10 minutes

TOTAL TIME
15 minutes

¼ cup unsalted butter

¼ cup olive oil

6 cloves garlic, minced

½ cup white wine, or chicken broth

Juice of 1 lemon (about 2 tbsp)

1 lb (450g) large uncooked shrimp, peeled and deveined

Salt and freshly ground black pepper

½ cup grated Parmesan cheese

¼ cup Italian breadcrumbs

¼ cup fresh parsley, minced

8oz (225g) linguine, cooked

Lemon slices, for garnish

1. Preheat the broiler to high.

2. In a medium oven-safe skillet over medium heat, heat the butter and olive oil. When the butter has melted, add the garlic, and sauté for about 1 minute or until fragrant.

3. Add the white wine and lemon juice, and let simmer for 2 or 3 minutes or until it has reduced by half. Add the shrimp, and cook for 3 or 4 minutes or until they are almost pink.

4. In a small bowl, combine the salt, black pepper, Parmesan cheese, Italian breadcrumbs, and parsley. Sprinkle the mixture over the top of the shrimp, and broil for 2 or 3 minutes until the topping starts to brown. Serve over hot linguine, garnished with lemon slices.

FAMILY FAVORITE ALFREDO SAUCE

| SERVES 10 |

This homemade Alfredo sauce is simple, quick, and tastes amazing. The cream cheese gives it a creamy texture that coats pasta perfectly. My kids love it, and we all know they are the best critics!

PREP TIME
10 minutes

COOK TIME
5 minutes

TOTAL TIME
15 minutes

½ cup unsalted butter

2 cups heavy whipping cream

4oz (115g) cream cheese

½ tsp minced garlic

1 tsp garlic powder

1 tsp **Easy Italian Seasoning**
(page 263)

¼ tsp salt

¼ tsp freshly ground black pepper

1 cup grated Parmesan cheese

1. In a medium saucepan over medium heat, add the butter, heavy whipping cream, and cream cheese. Cook, whisking, for 2 or 3 minutes or until the butter is melted and the sauce is smooth.

2. Add the minced garlic, garlic powder, Easy Italian Seasoning, salt, and black pepper. Continue to cook, whisking, for 2 minutes or until smooth.

3. Add the Parmesan cheese. Bring to a simmer, and continue to cook for 3 to 5 more minutes or until the sauce starts to thicken. Remove from the heat, and toss with your favorite pasta. Store any leftovers in an airtight container in the refrigerator for up to 5 days. Reheat slowly, stirring, over low temperature.

To view on device

BROWN SUGAR–GLAZED SALMON

| SERVES 4 |

This irresistible Atlantic salmon is glazed with a mouthwatering blend of sweet brown sugar and tangy soy sauce and then baked to perfection. It's a scrumptious supper dish that will have you reaching for seconds.

PREP TIME	COOK TIME	TOTAL TIME
5 minutes	30 minutes	35 minutes

2lb (1kg) salmon fillet (skin on or skinless)

2 tbsp olive oil

¼ cup packed brown sugar

¼ cup soy sauce

3 cloves garlic, minced

Juice of 1 lemon

1 tsp salt, plus more for seasoning

½ tsp freshly ground black pepper, plus more for seasoning

Sliced lemon, for garnish (optional)

Chopped fresh parsley, for garnish (optional)

1. Preheat the oven to 350°F (175°C). Line a baking sheet with foil.

2. Place the salmon on the prepared baking sheet, and season with 1 teaspoon salt and ½ teaspoon black pepper. Fold up the sides of the foil around the salmon.

3. In a small bowl, whisk together the olive oil, brown sugar, soy sauce, garlic, lemon juice, salt, and pepper. Pour the glaze over the salmon. Top the salmon with another sheet of foil, and seal.

4. Bake for 20 to 25 minutes or until the salmon is cooked throughout.

5. Switch the oven to the broiler setting.

6. Remove the foil from the top of the salmon, and baste with the sauce in the foil. Broil for 3 to 5 minutes or until the top is brown and caramelized. Garnish with lemon slices and parsley, if using, and serve.

To view on device

CREAMY TUSCAN GARLIC CHICKEN

| SERVES 6 |

This restaurant-quality recipe is ready in under 30 minutes. Browned chicken simmers
in a creamy garlic sauce that is full of sun-dried tomatoes and spinach. This hearty, flavorful
dish is delicious served over cooked pasta and will become an instant family favorite.

PREP TIME
10 minutes

COOK TIME
15 minutes

TOTAL TIME
25 minutes

2 tbsp olive oil

4 boneless, skinless chicken breasts
(about 1½ lb/680g), thinly sliced

1 cup heavy cream

½ cup chicken broth

1 tsp garlic powder

1 tsp **Easy Italian Seasoning**
(page 263)

½ cup shredded Parmesan cheese

1 cup baby spinach, chopped

½ cup sun-dried tomatoes, drained

1. In a large skillet over medium-high heat, heat the olive oil. Add the chicken, and cook for 3 to 5 minutes per side or until browned and no longer pink in the center. Transfer the chicken to a plate, and set aside.

2. To the skillet, add the heavy cream, chicken broth, garlic powder, Easy Italian Seasoning, and Parmesan cheese. Whisk over medium-high heat for 3 or 4 minutes or until the sauce starts to thicken.

3. Add the spinach and sun-dried tomatoes, and simmer for 2 or 3 minutes or until the spinach starts to wilt.

4. Return the chicken to the skillet, coat with the sauce, and warm through before serving.

To view on device

SHEET-PAN ROSEMARY PARMESAN CHICKEN
with Veggies

| SERVES 6 |

Sheet-pan recipes are so easy, and the result is roasted deliciousness.
Tender chicken breasts, coated in a flavorful blend of Parmesan cheese, rosemary,
and crunchy panko breadcrumbs, take center stage alongside perfectly roasted
veggies. This family-friendly meal will quickly become a dinnertime favorite.

PREP TIME
15 minutes

COOK TIME
30 minutes

TOTAL TIME
45 minutes

2 eggs

¼ cup 1% milk

1¼ cups panko breadcrumbs

1¼ cups shredded Parmesan cheese

2 tbsp chopped fresh rosemary

1 tbsp **Easy Italian Seasoning**
(page 263)

1 tsp garlic powder

4 boneless, skinless chicken breasts
(about 1½ lb/680g)

Salt and freshly ground black pepper

2 cups fresh green beans, ends
trimmed

1 lb (450g) baby Yukon Gold potatoes,
halved

1 red onion, quartered and separated

2 tbsp olive oil

1. Preheat the oven to 425°F (220°C). Lightly coat a baking sheet with cooking spray, or line it with parchment paper.

2. In a shallow dish, whisk together the eggs and milk. In another shallow dish, combine the panko breadcrumbs, 1 cup Parmesan cheese, rosemary, Easy Italian Seasoning, and garlic powder.

3. Season both sides of each chicken breast with salt and black pepper. Dredge the breasts in the egg mixture and then coat in the panko mixture. Lay the chicken on one side of the prepared baking sheet.

4. In a medium bowl, add the green beans. In a large bowl, add the baby Yukon Gold potatoes and red onion. Season the vegetables with salt and pepper, toss each bowl with 1 tablespoon olive oil, and sprinkle each bowl with 2 tablespoons Parmesan. Arrange the potatoes and onion in a single layer next to the chicken on the sheet pan.

5. Bake for 15 minutes. Flip over the chicken, add the green beans, and bake for 12 to 15 more minutes or until the chicken reaches an internal temperature of 165°F (75°C). Serve hot.

AIR-FRYER PORK FAJITAS

| SERVES 4 |

These sizzling pork fajitas are cooked in a flavorful seasoning alongside vibrant bell peppers and red onions. This recipe takes less than 25 minutes to prepare, and the fajitas taste like they're straight from a Tex-Mex restaurant.

PREP TIME
10 minutes

COOK TIME
12 minutes

TOTAL TIME
22 minutes

1 lb (450g) pork tenderloin, sliced thin

1½ cups sliced bell peppers, any color

½ cup sliced red onion

2 tbsp olive oil

3 tbsp fajita seasoning

Chopped fresh cilantro, for garnish (optional)

Small flour tortillas (optional)

1. Pat dry the pork tenderloin with a paper towel, and cut the tenderloin into thin slices to help it cook evenly. Add the pork to a medium bowl.

2. Add the bell peppers and red onion to the same bowl. Drizzle the olive oil over the top, sprinkle with fajita seasoning, and then toss to coat.

3. Transfer to the air-fryer basket, and cook at 390°F (200°C) for 12 minutes or until the pork is cooked throughout and no longer pink. Garnish with cilantro and serve with flour tortillas, if using.

To view on device

SKILLET SAUSAGE TORTELLINI
in a Roasted Red Pepper Sauce

COOKBOOK EXCLUSIVE

| SERVES 6 |

This flavorful dish combines tangy crushed tomatoes, roasted red bell peppers, and savory Italian sausage with fresh spinach and creamy cheese tortellini. A velvety smooth sauce made of heavy cream and Parmesan cheese finishes this Italian-inspired meal your family will love.

PREP TIME	COOK TIME	TOTAL TIME
5 minutes	20 minutes	25 minutes

1. To make the sauce, combine the tomatoes, roasted red peppers, water, garlic, kosher salt, basil, and oregano in a blender or food processor, and process until smooth. Add the heavy cream, Parmesan cheese, and sugar, and blend until incorporated.

2. In a large skillet over medium-high heat, cook and crumble the Italian sausage for 8 to 10 minutes or until no longer pink. Drain the grease.

3. Add the roasted red pepper sauce, tortellini, and baby spinach to the skillet, and cook for 6 or 7 minutes or until the tortellini is tender. Season with salt and black pepper, garnish with freshly grated Parmesan cheese and chopped basil, and serve.

1 lb (450g) ground Italian sausage

1 (9oz/255g) package refrigerated cheese tortellini, or your choice of filling

2 cups baby spinach

Salt and freshly ground black pepper

Chopped fresh basil, for garnish

FOR THE ROASTED RED PEPPER SAUCE

1 (14oz/400g) can crushed tomatoes

16oz (450g) jarred roasted red peppers, drained

1 cup water

1 tsp minced garlic

1 tsp kosher salt

6 fresh basil leaves, or to taste

½ tsp dried oregano

¾ cup heavy cream or half-and-half

¾ cup grated Parmesan cheese, plus more for garnish

1 tbsp granulated sugar

DESSERTS

If you have a sweet tooth like me, get ready for your new favorite section. Treat yourself to the addictive sweetness of **The Best Peanut Butter Bars** (page 225), a classic that has been in our family for years. Or indulge in the buttery goodness of **Browned Butter Pecan Cookies with Maple Glaze** (page 226). For seasonal delights, try the **Pumpkin Sheet Cake with Cinnamon Cream Cheese Frosting** (page 229) or the mouthwatering **Caramel Apple Slab Pie** (page 212). And don't miss out on the ultimate cookie bar, **The Best Carmelitas** (page 228), perfect for any occasion. This part is a paradise for dessert lovers, with plenty of recipes to make each meal's ending perfect.

◄ *If you are coming to my house for dessert, I will be making you cheesecake, for sure. This is one of my all-time favorite desserts, and I think it will become one of your new favorites!*

CARAMEL APPLE SLAB PIE

| SERVES 12–15 |

This twist on the classic apple pie is perfect for serving a crowd. The large-size slab pie has the same thin, flaky, melt-in-your-mouth crust; juicy apples; and crisp crumb topping you'd expect in a smaller, round pie and is generously drizzled with a rich and sweet homemade caramel.

PREP TIME
40 minutes

COOK TIME
45 minutes

TOTAL TIME
1 hour 25 minutes

3 ⅓ cups + ⅓ cup all-purpose flour

1 tsp salt

1 cup butter-flavored shortening

12 tbsp cold water

⅔ cup granulated sugar

1 tsp ground cinnamon

3 ½ lb (1.75kg) Granny Smith apples, peeled, cored, and cut into ¼-in (0.5cm) slices (10 cups)

FOR THE CRUMB TOPPING

1 cup quick-cooking rolled oats

1 cup packed brown sugar

½ cup all-purpose flour

½ cup unsalted butter

FOR THE HOMEMADE CARAMEL

1 cup packed brown sugar

4 tbsp unsalted butter

½ cup half-and-half

1 tbsp vanilla extract

Pinch of salt

1. Preheat the oven to 375°F (190°C). Lightly coat a 15×10×1-inch (38×25.5×2.5cm) baking sheet with cooking spray.

2. In a large bowl, combine 3⅓ cups all-purpose flour and the salt. Using a pastry cutter (or two knives), cut in the shortening until the mixture resembles coarse crumbs. Add 4 tablespoons cold water, and stir with a fork. Add the remaining water, 1 tablespoon at a time, until the dough is moistened. Use your hands to form the dough into a ball.

3. Turn out the dough onto a lightly floured surface, and roll it into a 19×13-inch (48×33cm) rectangle. Gently wrap the dough around a rolling pin, transfer it to the prepared baking sheet, and unroll the dough into the pan. Press the dough up the sides of the pan, being careful not to stretch it. Trim dough to ½ inch (1.25cm) beyond the edge of the pan, fold over the edge of the dough, and crimp as desired. Place the pan in the refrigerator to cool while you prepare the filling.

4. In an extra-large bowl, toss together the granulated sugar, remaining ⅓ cup flour, cinnamon, and Granny Smith apples until the apples are evenly coated. Carefully spread the apples evenly over the chilled crust.

5. To make the topping, in a large bowl, stir together the rolled oats, brown sugar, and flour. Using a pastry cutter, or two knives, cut in the butter until the mixture resembles coarse crumbs. Evenly sprinkle the mixture over the apples. Bake for 40 to 45 minutes or until the apples are tender. Cover the top with foil for the last 5 to 10 minutes if it starts to brown too quickly. Remove from the oven, and set aside to cool for 10 minutes.

6. Meanwhile, to make the caramel, in a medium saucepan over medium-low to medium heat, combine the brown sugar, butter, and half-and-half. Cook, whisking constantly, for 5 to 7 minutes or until the caramel begins to thicken. Remove from the heat, and stir in the vanilla extract and salt. Drizzle the warm caramel over the cooled pie, or let the caramel cool and store it in an airtight container in the refrigerator until ready to use; it will keep for about 3 weeks. Store any leftover pie in an airtight container in the refrigerator for up to 3 days.

To view on device

CHOCOLATE CHIP COOKIES

| SERVES 24 |

These classic chocolatey cookies get devoured in no time at our house. They're super easy to make, and they're so soft and delicious. You won't be able to resist having seconds!

PREP TIME	COOK TIME	TOTAL TIME
10 minutes	*8 minutes*	*18 minutes*

1. Preheat the oven to 350°F (175°C). Line a baking sheet with parchment paper.

2. In a medium bowl, and using a mixer on medium, cream together the butter, brown sugar, and granulated sugar.

3. Add the eggs and vanilla extract, and beat until fluffy.

4. Add the all-purpose flour, baking soda, baking powder, and salt, and mix until combined. Add the chocolate chips, and mix well.

5. Using a 1-inch (2.5cm) cookie scoop, drop the dough onto the prepared baking sheet. Bake for 7 or 8 minutes per batch.

6. Transfer the cookies to a wire rack to cool. Store any leftovers in an airtight container at room temperature for up to 5 days.

1 cup unsalted butter, softened

¾ cup packed brown sugar

1 cup granulated sugar

2 eggs

2 tsp vanilla extract

3 ½ cups all-purpose flour

1 tsp baking soda

½ tsp baking powder

1 tsp salt

2 cups milk chocolate chips

To view on device

SOFT AND DELICIOUS SUGAR COOKIES

| SERVES 24 |

Get ready to satisfy your sweet tooth with these irresistible sugar cookies. Made with a buttery dough and topped with a creamy frosting, these soft and chewy treats are the ultimate indulgence for any cookie lover.

PREP TIME	COOK TIME	TOTAL TIME
15 minutes	*10 minutes*	*25 minutes*

1. Preheat the oven to 350°F (175°C).

2. In a medium bowl, combine the all-purpose flour, baking soda, cream of tartar, and salt.

3. In a large bowl, and using a mixer on medium, cream together the butter, vegetable oil, 1¼ cups granulated sugar, confectioners' sugar, and water. Add the eggs, and mix well. Gradually add the flour mixture to the wet ingredients, and stir until completely combined.

4. Roll the dough into 1-inch (2.5cm) balls, and roll the balls in the remaining ½ cup granulated sugar before placing them on a cookie sheet. To give the cookies their signature rough edge, dip the bottom of a glass or flat measuring cup into the remaining sugar and press the cookie balls to flatten. You still want a thick cookie, so don't press them too thinly.

5. Bake for 8 to 10 minutes or until the bottoms are lightly brown. The centers should be barely baked because they will continue to bake as they cool. Be sure not to overbake or the cookies won't be soft.

6. To make the frosting, in a medium bowl, and using a mixer on medium, cream together the butter, sour cream, and salt. Add confectioners' sugar and milk to your desired consistency, add the food coloring to your desired color, and mix well. Spread the frosting over the cooled cookies. Store any leftover cookies in an airtight container at room temperature for up to 4 days.

5 ½ cups all-purpose flour

½ tsp baking soda

½ tsp cream of tartar

1 tsp salt

1 cup unsalted butter, softened

¾ cup vegetable oil

1¼ cups + ½ cup granulated sugar

¾ cup confectioners' sugar

2 tbsp water

2 eggs

FOR THE FROSTING

½ cup unsalted butter, softened

2 tbsp sour cream

1 tsp salt

4 cups confectioners' sugar

3–4 tbsp 1% milk

Red or pink food coloring

To view on device

CINNABON CINNAMON ROLL CAKE

| SERVES 16 |

This cinnamon cake, loaded with the comforting flavors of cinnamon and vanilla in a moist and fluffy sponge, is the perfect treat for any occasion. The sweet glaze adds the perfect finishing touch, making it a delightful dessert for friends and family.

PREP TIME	COOK TIME	TOTAL TIME
10 minutes	*25 minutes*	*35 minutes*

1. Preheat the oven to 350°F (175°C). Lightly coat a 9×13-inch (23×33cm) baking pan with cooking spray.

2. In a large bowl, and using a mixer on medium-high, combine the all-purpose flour, granulated sugar, salt, baking powder, milk, eggs, and vanilla extract. Slowly stir in the melted butter until combined. Pour the batter into the prepared baking pan.

3. In a medium bowl, mix the softened butter, brown sugar, and cinnamon. Evenly drop spoonfuls of the brown sugar–cinnamon mixture over the cake batter in the pan, and use a knife to swirl it over the cake.

4. Bake for 25 to 30 minutes or until a toothpick inserted into the center comes out nearly clean.

5. For the glaze, in a medium bowl, whisk together the confectioners' sugar, milk, and vanilla until smooth. Drizzle over the warm cake. Serve warm or at room temperature. Store any leftovers in an airtight container in the refrigerator for up to 3 days.

3 cups all-purpose flour

1 cup granulated sugar

¼ tsp salt

4 tsp baking powder

1½ cups 1% milk

2 eggs

2 tsp vanilla extract

4 tbsp unsalted butter, melted

1 cup unsalted butter, softened

1 cup packed brown sugar

1 tbsp ground cinnamon

FOR THE GLAZE

2 cups confectioners' sugar

4–5 tbsp 1% milk

1 tsp vanilla extract

To view on device

THE MOST PERFECT BROWNIES

| SERVES 16 |

Indulge in the ultimate chocolate lover's treat with this irresistible brownie recipe. Made with a blend of cocoa powders and a generous amount of chocolate chips, these fudgy brownies are a must-try treat.

PREP TIME	COOK TIME	TOTAL TIME
15 minutes + *30 minutes to cool*	*40 minutes*	*1 hour 25 minutes*

1 cup unsalted butter, melted

2 ¼ cups granulated sugar

4 large eggs

1 tbsp vanilla extract

1 ⅓ cups all-purpose flour

1 tsp salt

1 tsp baking powder

¾ cup cocoa powder

¼ cup dark cocoa powder

4oz (115g) chocolate chips or chunks

1. Preheat the oven to 350°F (175°C). Lightly coat a 9×13-inch (23×33cm) baking pan with cooking spray, and line it with parchment paper.

2. In a medium bowl, whisk together the melted butter and granulated sugar until well combined. Add the eggs and vanilla extract, and whisk until combined.

3. Into a separate medium bowl, sift the all-purpose flour, salt, baking powder, cocoa powder, and dark cocoa powder. Gently mix the dry ingredients into the wet ingredients until just combined. Fold in the chocolate chips.

4. Pour the batter into the prepared pan, and bake for about 35 to 40 minutes or until a toothpick inserted into the center comes out clean. If you like your brownies more on the gooey side, bake for 30 to 35 minutes.

5. Allow the brownies to cool for at least 30 minutes before serving. Pair with ice cream for a delectable treat!

NOTE

These brownies can be topped with crushed chocolate sandwich cookies, more chocolate chips, or chocolate candies if you love an extra punch of chocolate. For a darker brownie, use ½ cup regular cocoa powder and ½ cup dark cocoa powder.

To view on device

THE BEST NEW YORK CHEESECAKE

| SERVES 12 |

I have a deep love for cheesecake, especially New York cheesecake,
with its smooth, creamy decadence. It's perfect for any occasion, big or small, and
you can pair it with any fruit or flavor you want to make it different every time.

PREP TIME
1 hour + 6 hours to chill

COOK TIME
1 hour 40 minutes

TOTAL TIME
8 hours 40 minutes

FOR THE CRUST

1½ cups graham cracker crumbs
(about 12 crackers)

¼ cup granulated sugar

¼ cup unsalted butter, melted

Pinch of salt

FOR THE FILLING

2 lb (1kg) cream cheese, softened

1½ cups granulated sugar

8oz (225g) sour cream

5 large eggs

1 tbsp vanilla extract

1 tbsp lemon zest

1. Preheat the oven to 325°F (165°C). Spray a 9-inch (23cm) springform pan with cooking spray, place a circle of parchment paper in the bottom of the pan, and spray the top of the parchment with cooking spray.

2. To make the crust, in a medium bowl, combine the graham cracker crumbs, granulated sugar, melted butter, and salt until the mixture resembles damp sand. Pour the crumb mixture into the prepared springform pan, and press evenly, using the bottom of a flat glass or measuring cup to press the crumbs into an even layer.

3. Bake for 10 minutes. Remove from the oven, and allow the crust to cool completely.

4. To make the filling, in a stand mixer fitted with a paddle attachment or in a large bowl and using a handheld mixer, beat the cream cheese on medium-high for about 1 minute. Scrape down the side and bottom of the bowl, and beat for a few seconds more.

5. Add the granulated sugar and sour cream, and mix on medium-low until combined. Scrape the bowl, and mix for 10 additional seconds.

6. Add the eggs, and beat on low for 30 to 60 seconds or until combined. Scrape the bowl.

7. Add the vanilla and lemon zest, and beat until just combined. At this point, the batter should be smooth and somewhat runny.

8. Wrap the outside of the springform pan with four sheets of 18-inch (46cm) heavy-duty foil. (If you only have regular foil, add a few more sheets to ensure water cannot get into the pan.) Place the wrapped pan in a deep roasting or baking pan whose sides are at least 2 inches (5cm) deep. Pour the cheesecake batter into the springform pan.

9. Add very hot water to the roasting pan until it reaches about 1½ inches (3.75cm) up the outside of the springform pan. With the rack in the lower third of the oven, carefully transfer the roasting pan and cheesecake to the oven. Bake for 1 to 1½ hours.

To view on device

10. After about 1 hour, check the cheesecake's consistency. Slightly jiggle the pan—while it's still in the oven. The cheesecake should be jiggly but not liquid. If it still seems very liquidy, bake for 15 more minutes and check again.

11. When the cheesecake is firm yet jiggly, turn off the oven but leave the cheesecake inside with the door closed for another hour or so as the oven cools. Resist the temptation to open the oven! This allows the cheesecake to cool slowly and prevents it from cracking from the drastic temperature change between the hot oven and the much cooler kitchen.

12. When the oven and the cheesecake are cool, remove the pan from the oven and carefully remove the foil. Leaving the cheesecake in the pan, chill the cheesecake in the refrigerator for at least 6 hours

13. Before serving, run a knife around the edge of the pan to ensure an easy release when the springform is removed. Top with the desired toppings, and enjoy! Store any leftovers in an airtight container in the refrigerator for up to 3 days.

NOTE

If you are using whole graham crackers, use a food processor or blender to crush them into fine crumbs.

NO-BAKE CREAM CHEESE PEANUT BUTTER PIE

| SERVES 8 |

This peanut butter pie is easy to make and oh so good. A creamy, peanut butter filling sits atop a chocolate graham cracker crust and whipped cream and chocolate syrup add the finishing touch. You can make this pie ahead of time and store it in the refrigerator until you're ready to wow your guests.

PREP TIME	COOK TIME	TOTAL TIME
20 minutes + 2 hours to chill	*None*	*2 hours 20 minutes*

1½ cups chocolate or regular graham cracker crumbs (about 12 graham crackers)

¼ cup granulated sugar

6 tbsp unsalted butter, melted

8oz (225g) cream cheese, softened

½ cup confectioners' sugar

½ cup smooth peanut butter

8oz (225g) frozen whipped topping, thawed

Whipped cream, for serving

Chocolate syrup, for serving

Chopped peanuts (optional), for serving

1. In a medium bowl, combine the graham cracker crumbs, granulated sugar, and melted butter until incorporated.

2. Pour the crumb mixture into an 8- or 9-inch (20cm or 23cm) pie pan, and press firmly on the bottom and up the side of the pan to form the crust. Put the crust in the refrigerator while you make the filling.

3. In a large bowl, and using a mixer on medium, beat the cream cheese, confectioners' sugar, and peanut butter until smooth. Using a rubber spatula, fold in the whipped topping until combined. Pour the filling into the graham cracker crust, and spread to an even layer. Return to the refrigerator to chill for 2 hours or overnight.

4. Top with whipped cream, chocolate syrup, and chopped peanuts, if using, before serving. Store any leftovers covered with plastic wrap in the refrigerator for up to 3 days.

NOTE

To help the crust keep its shape, you can bake it before filling it. After forming the crust in the pie pan (step 2), instead of refrigerating the crust while you make the filling, bake it in a 375°F (190°C) oven for 8 minutes. Let it cool completely before adding the filling. Or to save time, you can purchase a ready-made graham cracker crust.

To view on device

EASY CHERRY PIE BARS

| SERVES 12–15 |

This cherry dessert is a heavenly blend of flavors. The buttery base is tender and indulgent, and the cherry pie filling adds a burst of fruity sweetness. Topped with a creamy glaze, these delectable treats will leave your taste buds wanting more.

PREP TIME	COOK TIME	TOTAL TIME
20 minutes	*35 minutes*	*55 minutes*

1. Preheat the oven to 350°F (175°C). Lightly coat a 15×10×1-inch (38×25.5×2.5cm) baking sheet or 9×13-inch (23×33cm) baking pan with cooking spray.

2. In a large bowl, and using a mixer on medium, cream together the butter and granulated sugar. Add the eggs, and beat well. Beat in the vanilla extract and almond extract.

3. In a medium bowl, combine the all-purpose flour and salt. Add to the creamed ingredients, and mix well.

4. Spread 3 cups batter into the pan, and spread it to an even layer. Add the cherry pie filling, and spread it evenly over the batter. With a small spoon, evenly distribute dollops of the remaining batter over the pie filling.

5. Bake for 30 to 35 minutes or until a toothpick inserted in the center comes out clean. Cool on a wire rack.

6. To make the glaze, in a small bowl, mix together the confectioners' sugar, vanilla extract, almond extract, and milk. Drizzle over the cooled bars.

7. Cut the bars into 12 to 15 pieces, and serve. Store any leftovers in an airtight container in the refrigerator for up to 4 days.

1 cup unsalted butter, softened

2 cups granulated sugar

4 eggs

1 tsp vanilla extract

¼ tsp almond extract

3 cups all-purpose flour

1 tsp salt

2 (21oz/600g) cans cherry pie filling

FOR THE GLAZE

1 cup confectioners' sugar

½ tsp vanilla extract

½ tsp almond extract

2 tbsp 1% milk

To view on device

PERFECT LEMON BARS

| SERVES 12 |

These classic lemon bars make my mouth water just thinking about them! The shortbread crust is topped with a tart, rich lemon center and finished with a dusting of confectioners' sugar. I love adding a little zest and small slice of lemon atop each square to make them stand out. I suggest doubling the batch because no one can eat just one.

PREP TIME
10 minutes

COOK TIME
40 minutes

TOTAL TIME
50 minutes

FOR THE CRUST

¾ cup unsalted butter, softened

⅔ cup confectioners' sugar

1½ cups all-purpose flour

FOR THE FILLING

4 large eggs

1⅓ cups granulated sugar

Zest of 2 large lemons (2 tsp)

Juice of 3–4 large lemons (⅔ cup)

⅓ cup 1% milk

3 tbsp all-purpose flour

Confectioners' sugar, for garnish

2 lemons, thinly sliced and seeded, for garnish

1. Preheat the oven to 350°F (175°C). Spray a 9×13-inch (23×33cm) baking pan with cooking spray.

2. To make the crust, in a large bowl, and using a hand mixer on medium, beat the butter and confectioners' sugar until blended. Slowly beat in the all-purpose flour.

3. Press the mixture into the bottom of the prepared pan. Bake for 18 to 20 minutes or until golden brown.

4. Meanwhile, make the filling by whisking together the eggs, granulated sugar, lemon zest, lemon juice, milk, and flour in a small bowl until frothy. Pour the filling over the hot crust.

5. Reduce the oven temperature to 325°F (165°C). Bake the lemon bars for 18 to 20 minutes or until the top is lightly browned. Transfer to a wire rack to cool completely.

6. When cooled, dust the top with additional confectioners' sugar, cut into 12 bars, and garnish each bar with 1 lemon slice. Store any leftovers in an airtight container in the refrigerator for up to 5 days.

To view on device

ZUCCHINI BARS
with Brown Butter Frosting

| SERVES 24 |

These cakelike bars are super moist and have shreds of zucchini throughout for extra veggie goodness. Add in some crunchy pecans and a creamy brown butter frosting, and you won't be able to resist these scrumptious bars!

PREP TIME	COOK TIME	TOTAL TIME
20 minutes	*40 minutes*	*1 hour*

1. Preheat the oven to 350°F (175°C). Lightly coat a 15×10×1-inch (38×25.5×2.5cm) baking sheet with cooking spray.

2. In a medium bowl, combine the all-purpose flour, baking powder, salt, and cinnamon.

3. In a large bowl, and using a mixer on medium, mix together the granulated sugar, vegetable oil, and eggs until smooth. Add the dry ingredients to the wet ingredients, and mix until incorporated.

4. Stir in the zucchini and chopped pecans. Spread the batter evenly in the prepared baking sheet.

5. Bake for 30 to 40 minutes or until a toothpick inserted in the center comes out clean. Remove from the oven, and cool completely.

6. Meanwhile, to make the brown butter frosting, in a medium saucepan over medium heat, heat the butter, whisking constantly, for 5 to 8 minutes or until it turns brown. Remove from the heat, add the confectioners' sugar, vanilla extract, and milk, and stir until smooth.

7. Spread the frosting over the cooled bars, cut into 24 bars, and serve. Store any leftovers in an airtight container in the refrigerator for up to 3 days.

2 cups all-purpose flour

1 tsp baking powder

½ tsp salt

1½ tsp ground cinnamon

1½ cups granulated sugar

1 cup vegetable oil

3 large eggs

2 cups shredded zucchini (about 3 medium zucchini, skin on)

1½ cups chopped pecans

FOR THE BROWN BUTTER FROSTING

6 tbsp unsalted butter

6 cups confectioners' sugar

1 tsp vanilla extract

8–10 tbsp 1% or 2% milk

To view on device

THE BEST PEANUT BUTTER BARS

| SERVES 16 |

This delightful peanut butter bars recipe was lovingly passed down to us by my boys' grandparents. It was a cherished staple in our household while they were growing up and one of the first recipes that made me fall in love with cooking. These bars are simply irresistible, and I am confident your family will adore them just as much as we do.

PREP TIME
10 minutes

COOK TIME
15 minutes

TOTAL TIME
25 minutes

1. Preheat the oven to 350°F (175°C).

2. In a large bowl, and using a mixer on medium, cream together the brown sugar, granulated sugar, butter, and 1 cup peanut butter.

3. Add the eggs, salt, baking soda, rolled oats, and all-purpose flour, and blend until combined.

4. Spread the mixture in an even layer on a 15×10×1-inch (38×25.5×2.5cm) baking sheet. Bake for 15 minutes—no longer—and let cool completely.

5. Spread the remaining ½ cup peanut butter in a thin layer on top of the cooled cookie bar. (I soften the peanut butter in the microwave so it spreads easier.)

6. For the frosting, in a medium bowl, combine the melted butter and cocoa powder. Add the confectioners' sugar, vanilla extract, and milk, and mix well. Spread the frosting over the top of the peanut butter bars. (If you let the frosted bars chill in the refrigerator for an hour, the frosting will set up faster.) Store any leftovers in an airtight container at room temperature for up to 4 days.

1 cup packed brown sugar

1 cup granulated sugar

1 cup unsalted butter, softened

1½ cups creamy peanut butter

2 eggs

1 tsp salt

1 tsp baking soda

2 cups rolled oats

2 cups all-purpose flour

FOR THE FROSTING

½ cup unsalted butter, melted

3 tbsp cocoa powder

1 cup confectioners' sugar

1 tsp vanilla extract

6 tbsp 1% milk

To view on device

BROWNED BUTTER PECAN COOKIES
with Maple Glaze

| SERVES 24 |

I love these cookies! They combine the rich flavors of brown sugar and pecans, creating a delightful crunch and caramel-like sweetness in every bite. The addition of the maple glaze is optional, but it adds a delicious flavor to this amazing cookie.

PREP TIME
25 minutes

COOK TIME
12 minutes + 1 hour to chill

TOTAL TIME
1 hour 37 minutes

1 cup unsalted butter

2 ¼ cups all-purpose flour

1 ¼ tsp baking soda

½ tsp salt

½ cup granulated sugar

1 cup light brown sugar

1 large egg

1 egg yolk

2 ½ tsp vanilla extract

1 tbsp sour cream

1 cup pecans, chopped, plus extra for topping

MAPLE GLAZE (OPTIONAL)

3 tbsp unsalted butter, melted

1 tsp maple extract

½ tsp vanilla extract

1 pinch salt

1 ½ cups confectioners' sugar

1. Line 2 baking sheets with parchment paper. Set aside.

2. Add the butter to a small saucepan over medium heat. Heat for 8 to 10 minutes, whisking frequently, until the butter begins to froth and become fragrant. Remove from the heat and let cool to room temperature.

3. In a small bowl, whisk together the flour, baking soda, and salt. Set aside.

4. Add the browned butter, granulated sugar, and brown sugar to a large bowl, and beat with a stand mixer or hand mixer until combined. Add in the egg, egg yolk, vanilla extract, and sour cream. Mix until smooth.

5. Add the dry ingredients to the wet ingredients and mix until combined. Fold in the chopped pecans by hand. Cover and refrigerate for at least 1 hour.

6. While the dough chills, preheat the oven to 350°F (175°C).

7. Use a cookie scoop to scoop the dough onto the prepared baking sheets, leaving about 2 inches (5cm) between the scoops.

8. Bake for 10 to 12 minutes or until golden brown. Remove from the baking sheet to a cooling rack.

9. While the cookies are baking, make the maple glaze, if using, by combining the melted butter, maple extract, vanilla extract, salt, and confectioners' sugar in a small bowl. Whisk until smooth.

10. Spoon or drizzle the glaze over the tops of the cooled cookies. Sprinkle chopped pecans over the glazed tops.

To view on device

THE BEST CARMELITAS

| SERVES 8 |

These heavenly cookie bars are utterly irresistible, with their buttery and chewy cookie base and generous layer of gooey caramel, and a sprinkling of rich semisweet chocolate chips.

PREP TIME	COOK TIME	TOTAL TIME
15 minutes	*30 minutes*	*45 minutes*

¾ cup unsalted butter, melted

¾ cup packed brown sugar

1 cup all-purpose flour

1 cup rolled oats

1 tsp baking soda

32 caramel squares, unwrapped

½ cup heavy cream

6oz (170g) semisweet chocolate chips

1. Preheat the oven to 350°F (175°C). Lightly coat an 8×8-inch (20×20cm) baking pan with cooking spray, or line it with foil or parchment paper.

2. In a large bowl, combine the melted butter and brown sugar. Add the all-purpose flour, rolled oats, and baking soda, and mix until combined.

3. Divide the cookie batter mixture in half, and pat one half into the bottom of the prepared baking pan. Bake for 10 minutes.

4. Meanwhile, in a small saucepan over medium-low heat, combine the caramels and heavy cream. Cook, stirring, for 10 minutes or until completely smooth. (The caramels can be melted in the microwave if you prefer. Heat only the caramels for 30 seconds at a time, stirring after each 30 seconds and being careful not to let them burn. Then add the heavy creamy to the melted caramels, and stir.)

5. When the cookie base has baked for 10 minutes, remove the pan from the oven and sprinkle the chocolate chips over the top. Pour the caramel mixture over the chocolate chips, and crumble the remaining cookie dough over all.

6. Return the pan to the oven, and bake for 15 to 20 minutes or until the edges are lightly brown.

7. Remove from the oven, and allow the bars to cool completely and the caramel to set before cutting and serving. (The caramel is *very* hot right out of the oven, so you want to let it cool. If needed, you can speed up the cooling process by putting it in the refrigerator for about 10 minutes.) Store any leftovers in an airtight container at room temperature for up to 1 week.

To view on device

PUMPKIN SHEET CAKE

with Cinnamon Cream Cheese Frosting

| SERVES 24 |

This moist and flavorful pumpkin cake is made with pumpkin purée and warming spices and is topped with a cinnamon-infused cream cheese frosting. It's perfect for fall gatherings or anytime you're craving a delicious pumpkin dessert.

PREP TIME	COOK TIME	TOTAL TIME
15 minutes	*25 minutes*	*40 minutes*

1. Preheat the oven to 350°F (175°C). Lightly coat a 15×10×1-inch (38×25.5×2.5cm) baking sheet with cooking spray.

2. In a large bowl, combine the granulated sugar, pumpkin purée, canola oil, and eggs.

3. In a medium bowl, whisk together the all-purpose flour, baking powder, cinnamon, baking soda, salt, and cloves. Add the dry ingredients to the pumpkin mixture, and mix well.

4. Pour the batter into the prepared baking sheet, and bake for 20 to 25 minutes or until a toothpick inserted in the center comes out clean. Remove from the oven, and cool completely.

5. To make the cinnamon cream cheese frosting, in a medium bowl, and using a mixer on medium, beat the cream cheese, cinnamon, butter, and vanilla extract until smooth. Add the confectioners' sugar, and continue beating until smooth. Spread the frosting over the cooled cake. Cover and refrigerate until serving. Store any leftovers in an airtight container in the refrigerator for up to 3 days.

1½ cups granulated sugar

1 (15oz/425g) can pumpkin purée

1 cup canola oil

4 large eggs

2 cups all-purpose flour

2 tsp baking powder

2 tsp ground cinnamon

1 tsp baking soda

¼ tsp salt

¼ tsp ground cloves

FOR THE CINNAMON CREAM CHEESE FROSTING

16oz (450g) cream cheese, softened

2 tsp ground cinnamon

½ cup unsalted butter, softened

2 tsp vanilla extract

4½ cups confectioners' sugar

CELEBRATIONS

This section is full of delightful recipes for every season and celebration. In spring, try the delicious **Irish Apple Cake** (page 232) and **The Best Egg Salad** (page 234). For summer, don't miss the **Creamy Ranch Poolside Dip** (page 240). Fall brings the spooky fun of Halloween with the **Halloween Charcuterie Board** (page 248), followed by Thanksgiving favorites like **Spatchcock Turkey** (page 244) and **Grandma's Famous Pumpkin Pie** (page 247). End the year by sipping on my classic **Traditional Wassail** (page 241) while gathered with the family by the fireplace. These traditional recipes are perfect for family celebrations all year round!

◀ *When friends and family get together, charcuterie boards are a must-make for me. You can count on a big charcuterie board filled with meats, cheeses, nuts, and fruit. There are so many fun and different ways to make a board. They are perfect for groups and so delicious to graze on all day.*

IRISH APPLE CAKE

| SERVES 8 |

This festive cake is perfect for celebrations all year long.
The apple cake is spiced to perfection, topped with a buttery streusel, and
drizzled with a warm custard sauce. It's a dessert you don't want to miss.

PREP TIME
45 minutes

COOK TIME
50 minutes

TOTAL TIME
1 hour 35 minutes

FOR THE CAKE

½ cup unsalted butter, at room
   temperature

½ cup granulated sugar

2 tsp vanilla extract

3 tbsp 1% milk

2 large eggs, at room temperature

1¼ cups all-purpose flour

1 tsp baking powder

1 tsp ground cinnamon

¼ tsp salt

3 large Granny Smith apples, peeled,
   cored, and diced

FOR THE STREUSEL

¾ cup all-purpose flour

¼ cup rolled oats

½ cup granulated sugar

¼ tsp salt

6 tbsp unsalted butter, chilled

FOR THE CUSTARD SAUCE

¾ cup whole milk

Dash of salt

3 large egg yolks

¼ cup granulated sugar

1 tsp vanilla extract

1. Preheat the oven to 350°F (175°C). Lightly coat an 8-inch (20cm) round cake pan with cooking spray.

2. To make the cake, in a large bowl, and using a handheld mixer with a paddle attachment, cream together the butter and sugar for about 2 minutes on medium-high or until light and fluffy. Add the vanilla extract, milk, and eggs, and mix well. Scrape down the side of the bowl.

3. In a medium bowl, sift together the all-purpose flour, baking powder, cinnamon, and salt. Add the dry ingredients to the wet ingredients, and mix until just combined.

4. Add the Granny Smith apples to the batter, and fold in by hand until evenly distributed. (This is an apple-heavy recipe, so it should be about 50/50 apples to the batter.) Pour the batter into the prepared cake pan, spread until smooth, and set aside.

5. To make the streusel, combine the flour, oats, sugar, and salt in a medium bowl.

6. Cut the butter into small cubes, and add to the bowl. Using your fingers, rub the butter into the dry ingredients, squishing the butter with your thumb and forefingers to flatten it and then rubbing it all together until you get the texture of coarse breadcrumbs. Evenly sprinkle the topping over the cake batter.

7. Bake the cake for 45 to 50 minutes or until the streusel is lightly golden brown and a toothpick inserted into the center of the cake comes out clean. Allow to cool for at least 15 minutes before serving with the warm custard sauce.

8. While the cake is baking, make the custard sauce. In a medium saucepan over medium heat, heat the milk and salt until steaming. Don't let it boil! It should be just barely to the point of simmering.

9. In a medium bowl, whisk together the egg yolks and sugar until pale and thick. This will take 2 or 3 minutes by hand or about 30 seconds if you use a hand mixer on medium.

10. Remove the milk from the heat, and slowly whisk it into the egg yolk mixture to raise the egg yolks' temperature. When all of the milk has been whisked into the eggs, pour the mixture back into the saucepan, set over medium heat, and cook, constantly whisking, for about 3 or 4 minutes or until the mixture has thickened enough to coat the back of a spoon.

11. Remove from the heat, stir in the vanilla extract, and serve warm over the cake.

To view on device

THE BEST EGG SALAD

| SERVES 4 |

This recipe is a lunchtime favorite when spring rolls around. It's so creamy and full of flavors, including fresh dill. I love adding fresh herbs and spices to any dish, but they are really the star of the show in this egg salad. Add it on top of some fresh bread, and I have no doubt that this will become your go-to egg salad recipe.

PREP TIME
10 minutes

COOK TIME
15 minutes

TOTAL TIME
25 minutes

8 large eggs

¼ cup mayonnaise

¼ cup chopped fresh dill

2 tsp minced fresh chives

2 tbsp Dijon mustard

½ tsp salt

¼ tsp freshly ground black pepper

To view on device

1. Add the eggs to a large saucepan, and fill it with cold water. Set over medium-high heat, bring to a boil, and immediately remove the pan from the heat. Cover the pan and let the eggs stand for 10 to 12 minutes. Remove the eggs from the water, and let them cool.

2. Peel and chop the eggs and then add them to a medium bowl.

3. Add the mayonnaise, dill, chives, Dijon mustard, salt, and black pepper, and mix until combined.

4. To serve, spread on bread, or use with your favorite crackers. Store any leftovers in an airtight container in the refrigerator for up to 4 days.

FROSTED LEMONADE

| SERVES 4 |

If you're looking for a cold drink for a hot day, this lemonade will hit the spot.
With just four simple ingredients, you can create a sweet, creamy treat that's ready
in 5 minutes. It's refreshing and satisfying and perfect for any occasion.

PREP TIME
5 minutes

COOK TIME
None

TOTAL TIME
5 minutes

1 cup freshly squeezed lemon juice

½ cup granulated sugar

1½ cups water

4 cups vanilla ice cream

1. To a blender, add the lemon juice, granulated sugar, water, and ice cream.

2. Blend until smooth, and serve.

To view on device

FRESH STRAWBERRY PIE

| SERVES 12 |

This delightful strawberry pie is bursting with fruit flavor in a crisp and buttery crust.
The combination of fresh strawberries and sweet gelatin dessert creates a refreshing
and vibrant dessert that's perfect for warm-weather gatherings.

PREP TIME
30 minutes + 3 hours to set

COOK TIME
25 minutes

TOTAL TIME
3 hours, 55 minutes

1 (9-in/23cm) ready-made piecrust, or piecrust from **Grandma's Famous Pumpkin Pie** (page 247)

2 tbsp cornstarch

¾ cup granulated sugar

1 cup water

1 (3oz/85g) package instant strawberry gelatin dessert

4 cups sliced fresh strawberries

1. Preheat the oven according to the type of crust used (see step 2).

2. If using a ready-made piecrust, bake according to the package directions. Cool completely before filling.

   If using the piecrust from Grandma's Famous Pumpkin Pie, preheat the oven to 425°F (220°C) and place the rack in the lower third of the oven. On a floured surface, roll out the crust dough to an 11-inch (28cm) circle, and transfer it to a 9-inch (23cm) pie pan, crimping the edge as desired. Prick the bottom of the crust with a fork several times. Place a large square of parchment paper over the center of the crust, ensuring it goes up the sides. Fill the crust with pie weights or dried beans, and bake for 15 minutes or until the edges begin to brown. Carefully transfer the parchment paper and pie weights to a plate to cool. Bake the crust for 5 to 8 more minutes or until the bottom is lightly golden brown. Cool completely before filling.

3. In a small saucepan, whisk the cornstarch, granulated sugar, and water until smooth. Bring to a boil over medium-high heat, and whisk for 2 minutes or until it thickens. Remove from the heat, and stir in the strawberry gelatin dessert until it's dissolved. Set aside to cool for 15 minutes.

4. Place the strawberries into the cooled crust, and pour the cooled gelatin mixture over the strawberries. Refrigerate for 3 hours or overnight until set. Store any leftover pie covered with plastic wrap in the refrigerator for up to 2 days.

To view on device

GRILLED HULI HULI CHICKEN

| SERVES 6 |

Huli huli chicken is a delicious Hawaiian grilled chicken dish. The chicken is marinated in a sweet and tangy sauce and then grilled and basted for a juicy and flavorful result. We love grilling this all summer long. It tastes great with my **Caramelized Grilled Pineapple** (page 151).

PREP TIME
10 minutes + 3 hours to marinate

COOK TIME
20 minutes

TOTAL TIME
3 hours 30 minutes

1 cup unsweetened pineapple juice

½ cup soy sauce

½ cup packed brown sugar

⅓ cup ketchup

¼ cup chicken broth

2 tsp grated fresh ginger

1½ tsp minced garlic

4 lb (2kg) boneless, skinless chicken thighs or breasts

Sliced green onions, for garnish (optional)

1. In a medium bowl, whisk together pineapple juice, soy sauce, brown sugar, ketchup, chicken broth, ginger, and garlic. Reserve 1 cup sauce for basting.

2. Add the chicken and sauce to a zipper-lock bag, place in the refrigerator, and marinate for at least 3 hours or overnight.

3. Preheat the grill to medium.

4. Remove the chicken from the sauce, and discard the sauce. Grill the chicken over medium heat for 6 to 8 minutes per side or until no longer pink. Baste occasionally with the reserved sauce during the last 5 minutes.

5. Garnish with green onions, if using, and serve.

To view on device

CREAMY RANCH POOLSIDE DIP

| SERVES 10 |

This dip is ideal for serving while hanging out by the pool or at any potluck. The cream cheese base and rich ranch flavor make it perfect for dunking veggies, potato chips, or your favorite crackers.

PREP TIME
10 minutes

COOK TIME
None

TOTAL TIME
10 minutes

8oz (225g) cream cheese, softened

1 red bell pepper, ribs and seeds removed, and finely diced

1 fresh jalapeño, finely diced (leave in the seeds for more kick)

1 (2.25oz/65g) can sliced black olives, drained

1 (15oz/425g) can corn, drained

1 (1oz/30g) package ranch seasoning mix (about 2 tbsp)

1. In a medium bowl, mix the cream cheese, red bell pepper, jalapeño, black olives, corn, and ranch seasoning mix until combined.

2. Serve immediately with your favorite veggies or chips, or store in an airtight container in the fridge for up to 24 hours.

To view on device

TRADITIONAL WASSAIL

| SERVES 8 |

Embrace the flavors of the season with this delightful holiday recipe. This simmering
warm drink of apple cider, citrus juices, and aromatic spices will transport you
to a cozy winter wonderland and is the perfect holiday crowd-pleaser!

PREP TIME
5 minutes

COOK TIME
1 hour

TOTAL TIME
1 hour 5 minutes

2 qt (2 liters) apple cider

2 cups orange juice

1 cup pineapple juice

10 whole cloves

5 cinnamon sticks

5 star anise pods

Pinch of ground nutmeg

½ cup fresh cranberries

1 orange, sliced

1 apple (your choice), sliced

1. In a large pot over medium-low heat, combine the apple cider, orange juice, and pineapple juice.

2. Add the cloves, cinnamon sticks, star anise, ground nutmeg, cranberries, orange slices, and apple slices.

3. Let simmer, uncovered, for at least 1 hour or all day. Serve hot.

To view on device

DAD'S FAMOUS MASHED POTATOES

| SERVES 8 |

This family recipe is always the star of our dinner table. Perfectly creamy and buttery, these mashed potatoes have been perfected by my dad, and I wouldn't change a thing. They have such an amazing flavor, and people are constantly begging him to make them.

PREP TIME
10 minutes

COOK TIME
15 minutes

TOTAL TIME
25 minutes

6 to 8 medium russet potatoes, peeled and cut into ½- to 1-in (1.25–2.5cm) cubes

Dash of salt

¼ cup 1% milk

½ cup unsalted butter

2 tsp seasoning salt

Freshly ground black pepper

Chopped fresh chives, for garnish (optional)

1. In a colander, wash the starch off the cubed russet potatoes until the water runs clear.

2. Add the potatoes to a large pot, and fill with enough cold water to fully submerge the potatoes. Add a dash of salt.

3. Set the pot over medium-high heat, bring to a boil, and cook the potatoes for about 15 minutes or until they are fork-tender.

4. Drain the potatoes, and add the milk, butter, seasoning salt, and black pepper. Using an electric hand mixer, beat the potatoes on high until they start to form peaks. (Or you can mash them with a potato masher.) Add milk if the potatoes still seem thick and need to be creamier and additional salt to taste. Garnish with chives, if using, and serve hot.

To view on device

SPATCHCOCK TURKEY

| SERVES 8–10 |

A spatchcocked turkey, in which the backbone is removed so the bird can lay flat, cooks faster and more evenly than an uncut turkey— it will be the most tender and juicy turkey you've ever made. I've included instructions for roasting in the oven and smoking.

PREP TIME	COOK TIME	TOTAL TIME
10 minutes	*1 hour 50 minutes*	*2 hours*

12–14 lb (5.5–6kg) turkey, neck and giblet bag removed

⅓ cup turkey seasoning

OPTIONAL GARNISHES

Fresh rosemary

Fresh parsley

Orange slices

Cranberries

1. Preheat the oven to 425°F (220°C).

2. Pat dry the turkey with a paper towel. Set the turkey breast side down on a wire rack set in a baking sheet. Using very sharp kitchen shears, cut along both sides of the backbone, from the tail to the neck, until it can be removed. Discard the backbone, or save it to make stock.

3. Flip over the turkey, and using your hands, press firmly to flatten the ribs. Be sure the turkey is completely flat, and push the thighs out flat on the baking sheet.

4. Rub the turkey generously with the turkey seasoning.

5. Bake for 20 minutes. Reduce the oven temperature to 400°F (205°C), and cook for about 1½ hours or until the thickest part of the turkey reaches 165°C (75°C).

6. Remove the turkey from the oven, tent it with foil, and let it rest for 10 to 20 minutes. Carve, garnish as desired, and serve. Store any leftovers in an airtight container in the refrigerator for up to 4 days.

NOTE

If you prefer to smoke your turkey, preheat the smoker to 240°F (115°C). Place the spatchcocked turkey skin side up in the smoker. Smoke for 4 hours or until the thickest part reaches 165°F (75°C).

To view on device

CRANBERRY PECAN BRIE BITES

| SERVES 6–8 |

There's something special about having a delicious little handheld appetizer to pass out at holiday parties. These bites layer pecans and soft brie, are topped with cranberry sauce, and are cupped in a flaky, golden brown crescent roll shell. The flavors melt together into the most delightful holiday treat. You won't be able to stop at just one!

PREP TIME	COOK TIME	TOTAL TIME
5 minutes	*15 minutes*	*20 minutes*

1 (8oz/225g) can crescent roll dough

½ cup chopped pecans

1 (8oz/225g) wheel Brie cheese, cut into 1-in (2.5cm) cubes

½ cup cranberry sauce

Sprigs of rosemary, cut into about 1-in (2.5cm) pieces, for garnish

To view on device

1. Preheat the oven to 375°F (190°C).

2. On a floured surface, roll out the crescent dough, pinching the seams to make one large square of dough. Cut the dough into 24 equal-size squares, and press 1 square into each cup of a nonstick mini-muffin tin.

3. Add about 1 teaspoon chopped pecans to the bottom of each cup, and press 1 Brie cube on the pecans. Top each with a dollop of cranberry sauce.

4. Bake for about 15 minutes or until the cups are golden brown. Garnish each with a piece of rosemary, and serve.

GRANDMA'S FAMOUS PUMPKIN PIE

| SERVES 8 |

My grandma was an amazing cook but an even better baker. I don't know anyone who could make superior bread, cookies, or pies to hers. But her pies were the *best*. This pumpkin pie graces our Thanksgiving table every single year, and it's just as beautiful as it is delicious.

PREP TIME	COOK TIME	TOTAL TIME
20 minutes	*1 hour 5 minutes*	*1 hour 25 minutes*

1. Preheat the oven to 425°F (220°C).

2. In a medium bowl, stir together the flour and ¼ teaspoon salt. Using a pastry blender, cut in the shortening until it's pea size.

3. Sprinkle in the cold water, 1 tablespoon at a time, tossing with a fork after each addition. Push the moistened dough to the side, and mix until all the flour is moistened. (Don't mix too much, or the crust will be hard.) Form the dough into a ball.

4. On a floured surface, roll out the dough, turning and flouring it a few times, until it is an 11-inch (28cm) circle. Place the dough in a 9-inch (23cm) pie pan, crimping the edge as desired.

5. In a large bowl, combine the granulated sugar, cinnamon, remaining ½ teaspoon salt, ginger, and cloves. Add the eggs, pumpkin purée, and evaporated milk, and mix until fully combined. Pour the pumpkin mixture into the prepared piecrust.

6. Bake for 15 minutes. Reduce the heat to 350°F (175°C), and bake for 40 to 50 more minutes or until a toothpick inserted in the center comes out clean.

7. Remove from the oven and cool on a wire rack for 2 hours. Serve, topped with the pecans and whipped cream, if using. Store any leftovers covered with foil in the refrigerator for up to 4 days.

1¼ cups all-purpose flour

¾ tsp salt

⅓ cup shortening

4–5 tbsp cold water

¾ cup granulated sugar

1 tsp ground cinnamon

½ tsp ground ginger

¼ tsp ground cloves

2 large eggs, slightly beaten

1 (15oz/425g) can pumpkin purée

1 (12oz/340g) can evaporated milk

Pecans, for garnish (optional)

Whipped cream, for garnish (optional)

NOTE

If you want to decorate your pie with piecrust leaves (or any other shape), first double the recipe. Preheat the oven to 350°F (175°C), and line a baking sheet with parchment paper or spray it with cooking spray. After making a piecrust with half of the dough, roll out the other half to about ⅛ inch (3mm) thick, and use leaf-shape cookie cutters to cut out dough leaves. Lightly brush each leaf with a mixture of 2 beaten eggs and 1 (12oz/340g) can evaporated milk. Place the leaves on the prepared baking sheet, and bake for 6 to 8 minutes or until lightly browned. Cool completely on a wire rack before adding them atop your cooked pie.

To view on device

HALLOWEEN CHARCUTERIE BOARD

| SERVES 8 |

This charcuterie board is a ghoulish treat for any Halloween get-together.
A spooky twist on your classic cheese board, it's filled with fruit, meat, spreads,
and nuts and is sure to be everyone's favorite snack at the party.

PREP TIME
30 minutes

COOK TIME
None

TOTAL TIME
30 minutes

CHEESE
12oz (340g) double cream Brie
12oz (340g) green goddess gouda
12oz (340g) blueberry vanilla
   goat cheese
14oz (400g) Merlot BellaVitano
Smoked gouda (for the "Boo" letters)

SPREADS
¼ cup apricot jam
Honey
¼ cup pesto

MEAT
6oz (170g) Prosciutto di Parma
15oz (425g) Italian dry salami

FRUIT
Strawberries
Seedless black grapes
Blackberries
Blueberries
Dried apricots
Fresh figs
Kiwi fruit
½ cup green olives

CRACKERS
Festive holiday crackers

CANDY
Individually wrapped chocolates

NUTS
Pistachio nuts

1. Start assembling your board by adding the cheeses to a large cutting board. Cut a pumpkin shape into the Brie wheel, and fill it with apricot jam.

2. Next, add the honey and pesto in small serving containers.

3. Add the green olives to a small bowl, and place it on the board.

4. Add in the meats and then the rest of the fruit.

5. Fill the rest of the board with pistachio nuts.

To view on device

AUTUMN CHARCUTERIE BOARD

| SERVES 8 |

This fall charcuterie board is a nice way to make any seasonal or holiday gathering special. It's packed with colorful and delicious food, comes together easily when you have all your ingredients ready to go, and will be a hit with all guests.

PREP TIME
15 minutes

COOK TIME
None

TOTAL TIME
15 minutes

DIP
Pumpkin dip or marshmallow dip

CHEESE
Cranberry goat cheese

Dutch spicy kaas cheese (green, red, and white square cheese)

Creamy Toscano cheese

Beemster cheese

MEAT
Italian dry salami

Peppered salami

Proscuitto

FRUIT
Sliced strawberries

Seedless red globe grapes

Green apple slices

Blueberries

Blackberries

CRACKERS AND COOKIES
Pumpkin cranberry crisps (Trader Joe's recommended)

Pumpkin-flavored sandwich cookies

Pumpkin spice batons (Pirouette recommended)

CANDY
Individual caramels

DECORATIONS
Small decorative pumpkins

Your choice of other fall decorations

1. Start assembling your board by placing the bowl of your choice of dip and any small pumpkins on a large round cutting board. Then add the cheeses.

2. Next add the salamis and prosciutto.

3. Add the fruit.

4. Fill the rest of the board with the crackers, cookies, candy, and other decorations.

To view on device

VEGGIE CHARCUTERIE BOARD

| SERVES 10 |

Every get-together needs a veggie charcuterie board full of colorful, beautifully displayed vegetables. Perfect as an appetizer or side dish, this nutritious fresh veggie board is always a hit.

PREP TIME
20 minutes

COOK TIME
None

TOTAL TIME
20 minutes

VEGETABLES

1 bell pepper, any color

Mini sweet peppers

Sugar snap peas

Radishes, cut into lilies

Celery, cut into 3-in (7.5cm) sticks

Broccoli florets

Cucumber slices

Cauliflower florets

Rainbow baby carrots

Rainbow cherry tomatoes

DIPS

Veggie dip or ranch dressing

Plain hummus, sprinkled with **Everything Bagel Seasoning** (page 264)

Beet hummus

1. Cut off the top of the bell pepper, and remove the ribs and seeds. Fill the pepper with the veggie dip or ranch dressing.

2. Start assembling your board by adding the filled pepper to a large cutting board.

3. Add small bowls of both kinds of hummus to the board.

4. Place the remaining vegetables around the dip and hummus bowls, and fill any holes with cherry tomatoes.

To view on device

BREAKFAST CHARCUTERIE BOARD

| SERVES 8 |

Wake up your family or guests with a delightful variety for breakfast.
Filled with everyone's favorite breakfast indulgences of waffles, pancakes, bagels,
fruit, and decadent toppings, everyone will love this unique board.

PREP TIME
20 minutes

COOK TIME
None

TOTAL TIME
20 minutes

BREADS

Mini pancakes, homemade or
   store-bought

Belgian waffles, homemade or
   store-bought

Mini bagels

SYRUP, SPREADS, AND SWEETS

Cookie butter

Chocolate hazelnut spread

Whipped cream

Maple syrup

White chocolate chips

Semisweet chocolate chips

Butter pats or slices

FRUIT

Bananas

Blackberries

Blueberries

Strawberries

Raspberries

1. Start assembling your board by adding the mini pancakes, Belgian waffles, and mini bagels to a large cutting board.

2. Add small bowls of cookie butter, chocolate hazelnut spread, and whipped cream, and add a small pitcher of maple syrup.

3. Add small piles of white and semisweet chocolate chips and butter pats.

4. Fill in the empty spaces with fruit.

To view on device

CHRISTMAS WREATH CHARCUTERIE BOARD

| SERVES 8 |

This wreath isn't meant to be hung on your door ... it's meant to be eaten! This Christmas charcuterie board is the perfect festive touch to any holiday party. It's stunning and delicious.

PREP TIME
20 minutes

COOK TIME
None

TOTAL TIME
20 minutes

CHEESES
English cheddar cheese
Cranberry cheese
Cranberry cinnamon goat's milk cheese
Garlic-herb Brie

MEAT
Italian dry salami

FRUIT
Strawberries
Seedless red grapes
Pomegranate seeds
Cranberries
Blueberries

SPREADS
Honey

NUTS
Pistachios
Candied pecans

CHOCOLATE AND CRACKERS
Peppermint bark squares (Ghiradelli recommended)
Baked crackers (any kind)

HERBS
Rosemary sprigs

1. Start assembling your board by adding the cheeses to a large cutting board.

2. Add the meat. (I arranged the salami slices like a flower and tucked them into small bowls.)

3. Add the fruit.

4. Add a small jar of honey, to the board or served alongside.

5. Fill the board with nuts, chocolate, and crackers.

6. Use some sprigs of rosemary in the center to outline the wreath, and tuck in some more along the outside edges.

NOTE

Use a star cookie cutter to cut out the center of the wheel of Brie and then spoon some of the pomegranate seeds into the hole. Add the star-shape piece of Brie as decoration elsewhere on the wreath.

To view on device

SEASONINGS & SAUCES

Get ready to enhance your recipes with a collection of my favorite homemade seasonings and sauces. Take your dishes to the next level with classic seasonings like **The Best Homemade Taco Seasoning** (page 265), **Easy Italian Seasoning** (page 263), and **Everything Bagel Seasoning** (page 264). Discover the incredible **World's Best Steak Marinade** (page 260), created by my talented son and guaranteed to make any steak insanely delicious. You've got to try my unforgettable **Famous Fry Sauce** (page 264), the perfect accompaniment to burgers and fries.

◀ *Homemade marinara is a staple recipe every week in our house. It is easy enough to make from scratch and perfect served with a big ol' bowl of spaghetti!*

WORLD'S BEST STEAK MARINADE

| MAKES 1½ CUPS |

When steak is cooked correctly, it is insanely delicious. With this marinade,
I have created a foolproof way of guaranteeing your steak will taste heavenly. It is
the perfect blend of spices and herbs to enhance the natural flavor of steak without
being overpowering and ensure your meat turns out perfectly tender every time.

PREP TIME	COOK TIME	TOTAL TIME
5 minutes	*None*	*5 minutes*

⅓ cup soy sauce

⅓ cup freshly squeezed lemon juice

½ cup olive oil

¼ cup Worcestershire sauce

1 tbsp minced garlic

2 tbsp **Easy Italian Seasoning**
(page 263)

½ tsp salt

1 tsp freshly ground black pepper

Pinch of crushed red pepper flakes

1. In a small bowl, whisk together the soy sauce, lemon juice, olive oil, Worcestershire sauce, minced garlic, Easy Italian Seasoning, salt, black pepper, and crushed red pepper flakes.

2. Use immediately or store in an airtight container in the refrigerator for up to 2 days.

NOTE

This recipe makes enough marinade to cover between two and four 10- to 12-ounce (285g–340g) steaks. To use, add your steak(s) to a large zipper-lock bag or a large bowl, and pour the marinade over the top. Marinate in the refrigerator for 2 hours or overnight before removing the steak to cook and discarding any remaining marinade.

To view on device

SPICY SRIRACHA MAYO

| MAKES 1½ CUPS |

Sriracha mayo is the condiment you'll want to put on everything!
I use it as a dipping sauce for anything fried or pair it with sushi, fish, or any
Asian-inspired dish. It's creamy and savory, with spice that packs a punch.

PREP TIME
5 minutes

COOK TIME
None

TOTAL TIME
5 minutes

¾ cup mayonnaise

4 tbsp sriracha sauce

2 tsp honey or agave (optional)

1 tbsp lemon juice or lime juice

1 clove garlic, pressed or minced

¼ tsp cayenne or chili powder

1. In a medium bowl, whisk together the mayonnaise, sriracha sauce, honey, if using, lemon juice, garlic, and cayenne until well blended.

2. Store any leftovers in an airtight container in the refrigerator for up to 5 days.

To view on device

HOMEMADE MARINARA SAUCE

| MAKES 2 CUPS |

This from-scratch marinara sauce is so easy and delicious and can be whipped up in under 25 minutes. It's perfect as a dipping sauce for bread or nestled on top of your favorite pasta.

PREP TIME
5 minutes

COOK TIME
17 minutes

TOTAL TIME
23 minutes

1 small yellow onion, finely diced

2 tbsp olive oil

2 (15oz/425g) cans stewed tomatoes

1 (6oz/170g) can tomato paste

1 tbsp **Easy Italian Seasoning** (page 263)

3 cloves garlic, minced

1 tsp salt

¼ tsp freshly ground black pepper

1 tbsp granulated sugar

½ cup chicken broth (or water)

To view on device

1. In a medium saucepan over medium-high heat, sauté the yellow onion in the olive oil for 5 to 7 minutes or until tender.

2. In a food processor or blender, pulse together the stewed tomatoes, tomato paste, Easy Italian Seasoning, garlic, salt, black pepper, and granulated sugar until smooth.

3. Add the tomato mixture to the saucepan, and stir in the chicken broth. Sauté for 10 minutes to let the flavors blend.

4. Store any leftovers in an airtight container in the refrigerator for up to 5 days.

EASY ITALIAN SEASONING

| MAKES 4 TABLESPOONS |

Use this homemade Italian seasoning in marinades and sauces, as a seasoning for meats and veggies, and even in salad dressings. The uses for this flavorful mix are endless.

PREP TIME
5 minutes

COOK TIME
None

TOTAL TIME
5 minutes

2 tbsp dried basil

2 tbsp dried oregano

1 tbsp dried rosemary

½ tbsp dried marjoram

½ tbsp dried thyme

To view on device

1. In a small bowl, combine the basil, oregano, rosemary, marjoram, and thyme.

2. Store in a tightly sealed jar in a cool, dry place away from direct sunlight for up to 6 months.

FAMOUS FRY SAUCE

| MAKES 2 CUPS |

This sauce is a classic in my home state of Utah, and trust me, once
you try it, you'll use it on *everything*. It's a delicious mixture of creamy textures
and flavors and is perfect as a dip for crispy fries or topping on a burger.

PREP TIME
5 minutes

COOK TIME
None

TOTAL TIME
5 minutes

1 cup mayonnaise

¾ cup ketchup

1 tsp Worcestershire sauce

1 tbsp pickle brine

1 tsp sweet paprika

Pinch of cayenne

1. In a small bowl, combine the mayonnaise, ketchup, Worcestershire sauce, pickle brine, sweet paprika, and cayenne.

2. Store any leftovers in an airtight container in the refrigerator for up to 5 days.

To view on device

EVERYTHING BAGEL SEASONING

| MAKES 10 TABLESPOONS |

This is one of my favorite seasoning blends. It's perfect for everything from avocado toast to sautéed
vegetables and adds the perfect punch of flavor and texture to just about anything.

PREP TIME
5 minutes

COOK TIME
None

TOTAL TIME
5 minutes

3 tbsp white sesame seeds

2 tbsp black sesame seeds

1½ tbsp poppy seeds

2 tbsp dried minced garlic

2 tbsp dried minced onion

1 tsp coarse sea salt

1. In a small bowl, combine the white sesame seeds, black sesame seeds, poppy seeds, dried garlic, dried onion, and sea salt.

2. Store in a tightly sealed jar in a cool, dry place away from direct sunlight for up to 6 months.

To view on device

THE BEST HOMEMADE TACO SEASONING

| MAKES 4 TABLESPOONS |

With the perfect amount of flavor and spice, this taco seasoning elevates just about any Mexican dish!

PREP TIME
5 minutes

COOK TIME
None

TOTAL TIME
5 minutes

1 tbsp chili powder

¼ tsp garlic powder

¼ tsp onion powder

¼ tsp dried oregano

½ tsp sweet paprika

1½ tsp ground cumin

1 tsp salt

1 tsp freshly ground black pepper

1. In a small bowl, combine the chili powder, garlic powder, onion powder, oregano, sweet paprika, cumin, salt, and black pepper.

2. Store in a tightly sealed jar in a cool, dry place away from direct sunlight for up to 6 months.

NOTE

I use 2 tablespoons seasoning for 1 pound (450g) ground meat.

To view on device

INDEX

ABOUT THE AUTHOR

Alyssa Rivers, also known as The Recipe Critic, is a beloved food blogger at therecipecritic.com, where she brings more than a decade of cooking experience to the table.

What started as a desire to help her family and friends cook delicious yet simple meals has grown into one of the most successful food blogs today. Alyssa's website has become a trusted hub for flavorful and approachable recipes tailored to busy families.

Recognizing the demands of a hectic lifestyle, Alyssa crafts quick, easy, and mouthwatering dishes using everyday pantry ingredients that even picky eaters will love. Whether it's a 30-minute one-pot wonder or a make-ahead casserole, her recipes provide efficient and family-friendly options that save time without compromising taste.

With *The Recipe Critic* and *The Tried & True Cookbook* as go-to recipe sources, busy families can savor homemade, nourishing meals while creating cherished memories together.